PAT ANSWERS

PAT HURLEY

WORD PUBLISHING

Dallas · London · Sydney · Singapore

Library of Congress Cataloging in Publication Data

Hurley, Pat, 1948–
  Pat answers.

  1. Teenagers—Religious life—Miscellanea. 2. Christian life—Miscellanea. I. Title.
BV4531.2.H845 1989   248.8′3   89-8915
ISBN 0-8499-3145-2

9 8 0 1 2 3 9 BKC 9 8 7 6 5 4 3 2 1

Printed in the United States of America

To
Corie Elizabeth

"May your questions be answered
and your life be measured, not
by the opinion of man but by the
wisdom of God. . . ."

Contents

A Word from Pat

Dear Friend,

Thank you for considering this "personal" relationship in book form. It is my way of sitting in your room and being a brother to you.

As you have asked questions, I have tried to provide some answers. My suggestions are not always serious, but life is funny once in a while. I have tried to be honest, enjoyable, real, and committed to bringing you closer to God and to the life He created for you.

There are a lot of questions I did not have time to answer. There are a lot of questions you could have answered better than I could. There are a lot of questions that have more than one answer.

But you and I have to begin somewhere. So, here it is. From anorexia to zits, you and I will cover the whole thing. You will think I went to your high school, lived in your house, and went on your dates. For the record, I didn't, but Jesus Christ did, and He has some thoughts on how you could handle those situations a little better.

Besides, you and I need something to read in the bathroom . . .

Love,
Pat

Parents

and other endangered species

```
Dear Pat,

I keep hurting my parents by the
things I do and say. They've taken
me to counselors, threatened me
with jail, and kicked me out of the
house. Why do I keep disappointing
them?

                        Ungrateful
```

Dear Unger,

You keep doing it because you need something.
What do you need? It could be one of several possibilities.

You need unconditional love Maybe you keep
testing your parents' patience to see if they're going to
quit loving you. That would be the answer that you
dread. Maybe you're testing them to see if they'll
stand by you regardless of your circumstance.

You need to get rid of the pain That core of
shame inside you (read Rom. 5:12–14) is screaming to
be forgiven and removed. It's like a cancer spreading
through your attitudes. Your outward behavior tells
me that something inside needs to be healed.

You need to punish them This is a very hurtful
thing some people do. If you feel that they've hurt you
in some way, then you figure out ways to pay them
back. Have they really hurt you? If so, then tell someone and take that first step toward forgiving.

You need to trust God instead of yourself Right
now you're playing judge and jury instead of letting
Him take control of this situation. I suggest you sit
down with a strong Christian, someone you really
respect, and find out how to turn this anger into love.
I trust you.

Dear Pat,

My parents are divorced, and I live with my mom. She's so hyper. She won't leave me alone. Help!

Going Crazy

Dear GC,

We can't change your mom, but we can help you adjust to her frenzied ways. Here are a couple of thoughts.

Her guilt Is it possible that your mom doesn't feel very successful as a person because she didn't have a successful marriage? A divorce doesn't make a person a loser, but it can make her feel like a loser. In order to make up for that feeling, she may have to work extra hard as a mom to make sure she doesn't fail there, too. Guess who feels that extra effort from mom? Yep, you guessed it! So, in a way, your mom's hyperactivity is a cover-up for how badly she may feel as a person struggling with the feelings of past failure and the fear of future failings.

Your potential It also sounds like your mom wants you to avoid the mistakes she made, so she is pressing extra hard to protect you. This is not healthy for you. This makes you want to stuff her face into a baked potato until she quits repeating herself! Try this instead: "Mom, I know you care about me. I love you, too. You're a great mom. I think you would be a great wife to the right man. I don't want you to ever think of yourself as a failure. I need the same encouragement." And then learn to relax together.

Dear Baggy,

I want you to sit down with your parents and tell them exactly what you told me. Also tell them that your bags are packed and that you're ready to leave.

I believe you when you say that they don't want you. I don't know how often they say that. When people get angry, they can say very hurtful things. I'm sure you're not proud of some of the things you've said over the years.

How do we solve this? Do you want to get an apartment and buy your own groceries? Are you ready to get a job after school and work while your friends are playing sports and hanging out at home?

There is a time to do these things. You might be right. Someday you do need to get out on your own. Unless your folks have physically or psychologically abused you, I want you to do three things:

(1) tell them how you feel; (2) if they don't listen, call a relative who will help you talk to them (your pastor or school counselor may even be able to help); and (3) unpack your bags.

Dear Pat,

It sounds like you had a rough home life growing up. How did you survive it?

Similar Situation

Dear SS,

There are several things to remember as you struggle through a tough family situation.

Realize God loves and accepts you as His child If you're a Christian, you're not fighting this battle alone. The thing I remember most about my salvation experience was how close I felt to God. I sensed Him saying, "It's all right. Come home to Me now. The battle is over. I love you, and I will never leave you!" The Bible backed that up in 2 Cor. 4:7-10. Read it. Believe it.

Separate the two problems Your parents aren't perfect. They have their own set of problems. You're not perfect either. Realize where you need improvement. Your parents' divorce is not your fault. If they drink excessively, that is their problem, not yours. Keep the sets of problems separate. If you don't, you'll keep blaming yourself for things you haven't done.

Find a "second" home You need to be reminded by godly people that you're not the jerk you feel like at home. You also need to spend time around a loving family to see family life done right. Ask God to give you some families you can visit frequently.

Don't panic You'll want to do something hurtful from time to time. That's a natural reaction, not a godly one. Hold off and call a friend instead for understanding.

Dear Pat,

There's always tension in our house. My parents don't get along. What can I do?

Tight as a Drum

Dear Tad,

Tell your parents exactly how you feel about the tension. Don't shout or scream. Don't accuse them or be negative. Just sit down with them and say something like this: "I realize that things aren't perfect between you two. Because you aren't getting along, there's a lot of tension in the house. I don't like tension. It bothers me. I get upset because I realize you're fighting, and I don't want you to. Can we do *anything* to change this situation?"

Then sit back and listen to their response. They may not realize there's tension; they may be used to it. They may not be aware of how much it's affecting you; that's why you need to tell them. They may want to separate from each other for a while but are afraid to do so for your sake. They need to tell you what they plan to do about the tension in the house.

You and your parents deserve better than to be constantly upset. It is not the way God intended us to live. If it continues, then your folks need to face their real problems and consider going to a Christian counselor as a family to find out what's causing the tension in your home.

```
┌──────────────────────────────────────┐
```

Dear Pat,

My parents favor my brother over
me. It's so obvious. I can't do
anything right, and he can't do
anything wrong. What can I do?

The Ugly Duckling

Dear Ducky,

I understand *exactly* how you feel. I was never my parents' favorite either. It was difficult for me for a long time until I began to trust God with it. Here are my answers for you.

Realize that you are a child of God (Rom. 8:14–16) You're not a family person first; you're not just a physical person on this earth. You're a spiritual being. The relationship you need to be most concerned about is whether or not God likes you. He not only likes you, He *loves* you. He loves you! You! You! Totally. You don't have to compete with anyone else.

Parents have always played favorites It shouldn't surprise you that parents like certain children over other children. Mom and dad are human, and they don't have perfect feelings for each family member. It's very possible that they might like one of their children more than they like each other! It's not scriptural, but it's true nonetheless.

You play favorites Is there someone in your family that you like more than someone else? Be honest. It's okay to have better "chemistry" with certain family members.

Don't base your worth on human approval (Rom. 5:8–11) Family support is important, but it's not meant to replace your relationship with God. You're worth the best God ever sent, and He did that just for you, whether your parents love you every minute or not.

Dear Pat,

My dad won't express himself to me. He never gets personal. He won't say "I love you" or anything else like that. Why?

Hurting

Dear Hurting,

Your dad sounds a lot like my dad. Here are some reasons why our fathers may not be very "personal."

He may not know how Your dad may have been raised by parents who came from the "old country," which means that you don't show your emotions. You work hard. You show affection by doing things for your children. You're taught to be seen and not heard. So when you become a parent, you do the same thing to your children. It's the only type of behavior you understand.

He may find it hard to be personal Your dad may have the ability to be tender or sensitive, but he chooses not to do so. He may think it is a sign of weakness to be "open," and that may be something he doesn't want to do. Talk to your mom about that.

He may not realize your need I once talked to a man who was a vice-president of his company. I told him, "You're losing your children because they're afraid of you. Try to be more sensitive." He was very upset with himself. As a businessman, he was very capable; as a father, he didn't realize how much he was hurting his family. You may need to say, "Dad, I need more than your money. I need to hear 'I love you' once in a while, too." He won't know unless you tell him.

There are a lot of dads who're willing to spend money on their children, but they don't say "I love you." It doesn't mean they don't love you.

Dear Pat,

My friends have more privileges than I do. They get to do everything! My parents are so strict. What should I do?

No Rights

Dear Nori,

There's only one thing you can do: Change your thinking! Look at it this way. Jesus Christ could have had any privilege on this earth. He could have made millions of dollars, stayed out as late as He wanted, and gotten the keys to the family camel whenever He wished.

Yet, even as a teenager, He *totally* obeyed His parents! There was never a time in His life when He sinned even once. Why? Because He never expected privileges. He was content in all things. He never compared Himself and His life to anyone else.

Paul said, "Do not *merely* look out for your own personal interests, but also for the interests of others. Have this attitude in yourselves which was also in Christ Jesus, who, although He existed in the form of God, did not regard equality with God a thing to be grasped, but emptied Himself, taking the form of a bond-servant" (Phil. 2:4–7a).

If you "empty yourself" of all comparisons, all ego, all expectations, and all things you think you have a right to own, you won't worry about the privileges of others. Jesus has given you exactly what you need to lead a contented life. Pushing for more is only going to frustrate you.

```
Dear Pat,

My mom and I are always arguing
about my messy room. Any answers?

                           Exasperated
```

Dear Exa,

I understand both positions. Your mom wants to be proud of her home, and that includes every room in the house. She also wants you to have a room that reflects an orderly mind—not one that looks like the *Titanic* ten minutes after it hit the iceberg!

You can understand that, but it is *your* room. You need a place that's yours and yours alone. If you shared your room with a brother or sister, then my answer would be different.

As long as your room is not affecting the rest of your family—like odors that could stun buffalo or noises that could shatter human nervous systems—I believe you have the right to privacy in your room. You need and deserve a place that belongs to you. Adults have places where they can retreat from the pressures of life; I believe you have that right, too.

Sit down with your mom and ask her what *specifically* bothers her about your room. I'd like to see you keep it reasonably neat. You may even have friends trapped under those mountains of clothes. You never know! I hope she can respect your need for privacy. Just don't expect to have clean clothes every week or to be featured on the cover of *Architectural Digest!*

Dear Pat,

My parents are in the middle of a separation. I am totally depressed. I want them to stay married. What can I do?

Torn Up

Dear Torny,

My parents got divorced *twice*. It's a horrible feeling, but not a hopeless one. This is what I did:

Read Psalms every day Spend thirty minutes or so daily in this book. It'll encourage you so much to know that you're not alone. "The steps of a man are established by the Lord; and He delights in his way. When he falls, he shall not be hurled headlong; because the Lord is the One who holds his hand" (Ps. 37:23–24). There are a lot of great psalms like that.

Find a Christian adult to talk to Don't bury your feelings. What hurts you is something you need to talk about. Ask God to give you someone to go to when it gets bad . . . and talk! Get the "poison" out.

Don't blame yourself When two people decide not to love each other, it's not your fault. There's nothing you can do except pray for them. This isn't between you and them. It's their issue. Keep your head up.

Don't take sides You love them both, even with their failures. God doesn't ask you to favor one or the other, and neither should your parents.

Dear Pat,

My parents think they're always right. Do you have any suggestions on how I should respond?

Put Down

Dear Putsy,

Your parents aren't always right. No one on this earth is always right. There's only one Person who's perfect and without sin. His name is Jesus Christ. He's not one of your parents!

Here are some guidelines:

Do not confuse discipline with perfection It may seem to you that your parents think they're always right because you tend to remember arguments you've lost to them. If they make a decision to say no to you, don't focus on their being right; concentrate on the fact that they're doing it for your best interest. Figure out why they're saying no.

Ask yourself: "Do they love me?" Your question suggests a them-against-me mentality. Is that true? Are they winning arguments with you because they dislike you? Or are they making their choices based on their love for you? That's something you have to decide.

Explain to them how they come across to you Sit down with your parents when you're not arguing and tell them what you told me. Explain that you don't want to seem "100 percent right" to your kids someday, and that you can learn humility by seeing them demonstrate a little more. Be honest with them. They need to know how they're coming across to you.

```
Dear Pat,

My dad is a big leader at church,
but at home he's such a hypocrite!
I've lost all respect for him. What
should I do?

                    Really Disappointed
```

Dear Red,

The first thing you need to do is realize how much love you have for your dad. You obviously care about him very much. That's why you're so hurt now. Remember the love chapter from 1 Corinthians 13? "If you love someone you will be loyal to him no matter what the cost. You will always believe in him, always expect the best of him, and always stand your ground in defending him" (1 Cor. 13:7, LB). Put that on your mirror and read it every day. Put your dad on your prayer list.

You need to do one more thing. Do what my daughter did for me one day when I lost my temper. She started crying. I'm not asking you to shed any tears; I'm asking you to let your father know how much it hurts you to see him acting one way at home and another way at church. You could say: "Dad, I know you love Jesus Christ. You taught me to love Him, too. It hurts me to see you being phony about it. No matter what you decide, I will always love you. But we both deserve better than this."

Dear Pat,

All I ever hear about from my parents is grades, grades, grades! Why do they pick on me?

Burned Out

Dear Burnie,

Does the following conversation sound familiar? You bring your grades home and the conversation goes like this:

Burnie: Hi!
Parents: Did you get your grades today?
B: Yeah . . .
P: And?
B: Did pretty good . . . I got all "B's" except for one . . . "C."
P: (Ignoring all the "B's") Why'd you get the "C"?
B: Uh, it's a hard class. I don't understand volley-ball!
P: We'd be so proud if you could get *all* "B's".
B: Aren't you happy with what I've got now?
P: When I was your age, I used to walk eighty miles to school! In the snow! Barefoot! Uphill! Carrying my six brothers and sisters above my head!
B: Great! Here comes a blizzard. Why don't you go relive your childhood right now!
P: What did you say?
B: Nothing . . . Sorry. I can't ever please you.
P: Just get all "B's" . . . and then we'll talk about getting some "A's" . . . maybe *all* "A's" . . .
B: (Walking away) Yeah, right . . .

P: (To themselves) Remember when *we* got all
"B's" and one "C" . . .

If that communicates to you, then take comfort in
one fact: I've given this illustration to more than three
million students and parents, and they all applauded
furiously because *everyone* talks about grades! You're
not alone. You'll probably tell your kids about the
snow, too.

```
Dear Pat,

My dad is always criticizing me.
I can't seem to do anything right.
Even my mom agrees that it's not
fair. What's going on?

                        The Loser
```

Dear "Pat,"

I'm using my name to write back to you because
you're not a loser. Besides, I had a dad who always
criticized me, too. There could be several possibilities.

Your dad is an unhappy person If you put a
piece of limburger cheese on your nose, you'll think
the whole world stinks! It may never occur to you that
maybe the problem is inside. The way your dad gets
his hurt out is to dump it on you.

**You remind him of someone or something he dis-
likes** Next time your dad criticizes you, listen carefully to what he's griping about. He may recognize
one of his own faults in you, or your mannerisms may
trigger a negative reaction because of a person he
dislikes.

Your dad is showing "affection" The chances
are good that your dad has a hard time saying "I love
you" or paying you a compliment. He may have been
raised to only comment personally when something is
wrong. That's not your fault.

In fact, most of this may not be your fault. Your
dad may need to sit down with a counselor and see
why he hurts you. In the meantime, look for the clues
I suggested. Stop calling yourself a loser; neither one
of us is.

Dear Pat,
My parents are way too strict —especially my dad. I'm sixteen years old, and I deserve some trust. Do you have <u>any</u> suggestions?

On a Leash

Dear Leash,

Here are some things you can do to loosen the grip your parents have on you. Read Prov. 13:1-3 before you sit down with them.

Ask them if you've done anything to earn this restricted treatment Parents have memories like elephants. You do one thing wrong, and they think you may do it again sooner or later. Is there an issue that's not resolved between you and them? It's very important that you consider this possibility before you go on to the other options.

Your parents' upbringing is important If they had too much freedom from their parents and it hurt them in life, then they may decide to treat you in the opposite way.

Did they trust themselves when they were your age? It's possible they think that all sixteen year olds are not capable (or worthy) of personal responsibility. That's not true, of course, but their opinion is what they go on.

Compliment them Tell them you understand some of the restrictions. Work out a plan for more freedom. Tell them you appreciate what they're doing for you. Be sensitive and gentle here. Don't try to win an argument. Try to understand how to improve your disagreement in this area. Be patient with them, yourself, and the frustrating situation.

Dear Pat,

I'm a sophomore in high school. What would you suggest as a proper curfew for me?

                                            Jail Bird

Dear Jailed,

It's not a matter of curfew; it's a question of trust. It doesn't matter how old you are; it depends on how mature you are, or how mature your parents think you are.

I talked with several freshmen who responded to my questions on curfew almost unanimously. You might want to show this survey to your parents:

Curfew on weeknight: When we want to!
Curfew on weekend: By breakfast!
Curfew in summertime: Labor Day!

I think you get the idea. I don't think you want a chart on what the appropriate times are for your age group; you want to know how to extend your curfew. Right?

Always recognize your parents' authority You can disagree all you want, but they'll have the last word on when you're due home. Don't fight them.

Be honest Honesty builds trust. Trust extends curfews. Don't lie to them. Lie once, and you've set trust back months.

Always beat their curfew They want you home by 11:00 P.M.? Come in at 10:50. If they say midnight, be home by 11:45. When they see that kind of response, they'll trust you more. We know what happens next, don't we?

Dear Pat,

What do you think about Christian rock music? I know what my parents think about it, and it isn't very positive.

A Big Fan

Dear Fanny,

I think there is some great Christian music out there. I also think that some individual artists and groups should quit pretending they're ministering in the name of Jesus Christ. Here are some keys to recognizing music that God is blessing.

Their spirit off-stage (1 Pet. 1:15–16) If Christian musicians are always "on-stage," even when the concert is over, then they are living for the glory rather than their Lord.

Desire to minister (Matt. 15:8) If they think of themselves as ministers first and musicians second, that's a good sign. If they really do the work of a ministry off-stage, that's an even better sign!

Understandable words (Isa. 55:11) The Word of God through music has to communicate. If you can't follow what they're singing, the chances are good that they don't care. They need to care.

Actions on stage (Matt. 5:16) If they're selling sex, they're not selling Scripture!

Product emphasis (Exod. 20:4–5a) If their posters, t-shirts, and albums focus more attention on the group than on the God they say they serve, go to another group's table. This is the Lord's glory, not theirs.

Dear Pat,

Have you ever noticed some of the
funny things dads do?

Observing Son

Dear OS,

Yes, it's true. There *are* some strange things fathers do. Have you ever noticed the following?

Dads can sleep in any position at any time
Try to imagine a walrus who has died in an easy chair, lying there with his mouth open, snoring as though a freight train had just exploded through a straw! His coma continues *until* you change the channel on the television set. "Hey, I was watching that!" he bellows. "Turn that back to 'Aztec Art in the Wild Kingdom'!" Then the walrus goes back to sleep with a contented smile.

Dads tell dumb jokes to your friends This is very embarrassing. Not only does your dad tell jokes that no one understands, but they aren't even funny to those who do understand them. Then your dad laughs at his own joke and walks away saying something like, "Boy, that is so funny!" Meanwhile, you and your friends look at each other and say, "Where'd he get those jokes . . . K-Mart?"

Dads pretend they work around the house Follow them around as they "fix" things that somehow stay broken for years and years and years. Their favorite job is to move stuff from one side of the garage to the other . . . and then move it back again. This makes mom smile because she knows not to give him a *real* job!

Dads love clever phrases Of course you've heard the old saying "Do you think money grows on trees?" Dads love that one because they're fairly sure that money doesn't grow on trees. They also like motivating their teenagers with such zingers as: "No guts, no glory" and "As long as you live under **my** roof, you'll live by **my** rules!" My personal favorite is: "Don't you know there are children starving in Africa?!" I've always wanted to hand him an envelope filled with overcooked fish sticks and say, "Ship it to them." I knew those poor children in Africa would be gagging as much as I was when my mom laid those shriveled brown things on my plate. I wouldn't wish those on any continent.

Dads never ask for directions If you were driving from Ohio to Disney World and you cruised by the Golden Gate Bridge, would you think that you were . . . lost? Good chance. Would your dad admit it? No way! Would he stop and ask for directions? Only with a gun to his head! Would he tell you it was a shortcut? Yes, dads are so predictable.

Dads love remote control Your father probably doesn't watch television, he zaps it! Zap! "Less filling —tastes great!" Zap! "Tonight's movie is brought to you by . . ." Zap! "Do you have . . . Diarrhea?" Zap! "We believe God wants you to call in and pledge . . ." Zap! "Oh, Dirk, I can't handle this relationship . . ." Zap! "Do you know what spells relief?" Z-A-P!

It's also important to remember that dads do not realize that these things are funny. They think they are normal.

Dear Pat,

What are some of the funny things
moms do?

Future Mom

Dear FM,

Hold on to your seat belt! Here we go . . .

Moms ask dumb questions These are women
who may have a Ph.D., but once they become mothers, they forget all logic. They look at their child and
say something brilliant like: "Go get me something
to hit you with!"

This doesn't make a lot of sense, does it? How
many children are going to rush out and bring
back something that hurts! I used to bring my mom
a feather. "Hit me, Mom. I deserve it!" I would say.
That feather never bothered me much! Here are
some other classic mom questions that are no reflec-
tion on her intelligence under normal circumstances:

"Do you want your face slapped?"
"Are you home?"
"Are you going out dressed like that?"
"What do you think I am . . . Stupid?"

Just remember to respect her whether her questions make sense or not. She does have your best interests at heart, and the Lord wants you to look past
the emotion of the moment. With that in mind, here
are some more humorous "momisms":

Moms get everyone to think like they do Have
you ever sat watching television, completely relaxed
and comfortable? You weren't too warm or too cold,
were you? Then your mom suddenly appeared and

said, "Go put a sweater on." Were you cold? No. Why does she want you to get warmer? Because she's cold. So put on your sweater so *she* doesn't freeze to death.

Moms embarrass their children Remember when you were in the fourth grade? Who was it that came to your school, brought your lunch, and said in front of all your friends, "When you get home, pick up all your underwear"? Good old mom.

Or when you were playing outside with your friends, trying to be hip and "cool," and here comes mom with that voice that could melt Darth Vader's mask: "Get in the house *now!*" Remember how your friends smiled as you went home?

Or the time when you really liked a girl in junior high, and your mom met her and said, "Oh, so *you're* Wendy! You *are* cute!" Then *your* mom looked slyly at you and winked. Didn't you feel like dying!

Moms have answers for everything The following is a chart of your questions and your mom's answers. Every mom has this chart on her wall:

YOU	MOM
"Everyone's going but me!"	"Well, if everyone jumped off a cliff, would you?"
"Why?"	"Because I said so!"
"Is that the only reason?"	"I'm your mother!"
"What's wrong with tonight?"	"Tonight's a *school* night!"
"Why are you doing this?"	"I'm only doing this because I love you."
"You don't care about my feelings!"	"Believe me, this hurts *me* more than it hurts you!"

Forget it. You'd have better luck with Freddy Krueger in your wildest nightmare! Because I said so . . .

Dear Pat,

What qualities should a good mother have?

Wanting a Great Mom

Dear Wanny,

There are several traits that make a great mom. Here are a few that I've heard as I've traveled the country:

Understanding This is probably the most important quality. When no one else listens, mom is always there to understand you. Whether you cut your knee or bruise your ego, you need that smile and pat on the back that says, "Everything's going to be okay!"

Reality Dads may bluff a lot, but moms **always** tell you the truth. If your ears aren't clean, your pants are wrinkled, your blouse is transparent, or your language is too salty, you'll hear about it from mom. Moms won't pull any punches when it comes to cleaning up your act. That's because you're representing her out there.

Protection Ever seen your dad lose his temper? Who will usually step between you and him at that point? Yes . . . mom. Moms are born peacemakers. They have the gift of settling everyone down. A good mom knows how to use that gift well.

Insight No one figures out things better than moms. They can see through phony people, explain confusing situations, and define cloudy decisions. Whenever in doubt, throw a tropical storm their way, and they'll paint you a rainbow! It's a gift all women have, but one many never use.

Inner strength Do you know what really held the country together when President Kennedy was assassinated? It was the sight of his wife handling her emotions with dignity and character in the face of devastating pain. We all reasoned, "If Jackie can make it through this, we can, too!" I wasn't there when Jesus died on the cross, but I'll bet His mother demonstrated that same strength under pressure.

Familiarity There's something comforting when you walk in the house and see your mom. Dad could travel five days a week, but mom needs to be there. Just the sight of her standing in the kitchen with that look of hers is something that always brings a sense of security to our hearts. Do you know what I mean? Yeah, I thought you did. That's what we'll miss most about her.

Graciousness The chances are good that we're not going to learn this quality from our dad, our friends, our bosses, or from our celebrity heroes. We're supposed to learn it from the Word of God, but we'll probably realize it from our mothers. The ability to say things nicely, even when our heart is burning with anger and anxiety, is a gift from good mothers. Those mothers are a gift from God—a **gracious** gift from God.

Dear Pat,

What are the great qualities of a
dad?

Wanting to Respect Him

Dear Respy,

Dads with the following assets will always have
the respect of their children.

Consistency The number-one quality that
makes children feel secure is whether or not they
can trust their dads to respond as Christ would as
much as possible. Young people get very shaky
when they don't know how their fathers are going
to react. This is what brings tension to most homes.

Biblical standards You need to know what
Jesus Christ expects of you, and who can tell you
better than your dad? But if he is going to tell you,
he'd better start by telling himself first. Most young
people want rules and boundaries. They want to
know that they are being shaped by a father who
uses his own life as the chalk.

Freedom to fail Why do people fail repeat-
edly? They fail because they're afraid to fail. They
think it's more powerful than they are. Do you know,
Respy, what's greater than fear? *Perfect love.* A dad
who communicates perfect love whenever you think
you're failing will help you overcome that failure. A
dad who can say, "Sure, you didn't act perfectly in
this situation, but God and I love you anyway" is one
who will have your allegiance.

Confidence A dad needs to set some standards for himself and fight for them. You need (and
deserve) a father who believes God can do great

things in this world. A spiritually neutral father is not going to give you something you can emotionally embrace.

Patience   Read the Gospels and see the patience of Jesus Christ on every page. How many times could He have lost His temper with His followers and said, "That's it! You're all idiots! I'm finished with you!" But He never did. A father who can bite his tongue when he wants to bite off your head is a good one.

Sensitivity   There are things that are important to you, but they may not hold the same importance for someone else. But you're sensitive to them. A good dad will understand that and encourage you here. It's especially important for a man to be this way, because we tend to expect this quality only of mothers.

Sense of humor   Most young people love to laugh. A lot of adults out there have forgotten how to smile. Your dad needs to express himself in this area. It'll add joy to your relationship and years to his life.

Honors his wife   The most important thing teenagers want from their parents is for them to love each other. It begins with Eph. 5:25–27. You show me a dad who really puts his wife on a pedestal, and I'll show you the basis for a spiritually healthy family. It is the mark of a really great man.

Friends

How to like yourself despite what others say

Dear Pat,

I have a friend who's always insulting me. This usually happens in front of others. When it's just the two of us, my friend is pretty nice. Suggestions?

Seeing Double

Dear Seeing,

I had a friend like that in high school. In fact, we were best friends. Do you know what he signed in my yearbook? "To Pat—a funny-looking, dumb, ignorant idiot! Your friend, Vince." Can you believe that!

Looking back now, I realize he didn't understand the meaning of the word "friend." He was interested in making himself look good at my expense. No matter how perfect I tried to be around him, he would always cut me down.

Here are a few suggestions:

Realize your friend has a confidence problem People say things to hurt others because they hurt inside. That pain has to go somewhere. It usually goes to the one they care for the most.

Explain your feelings firmly You have the right and the responsibility to say, "Enough is enough. If I'm your friend, then start supporting me instead of putting me down. If you can't do that, then go find someone else to rip on. I deserve better than this treatment."

Don't play the game Once you've stated your position, leave it up to your friend and be as kind as you can when you're together. Demonstrate how a friend is supposed to act. If the situation doesn't improve, then make new friends. You haven't lost a friend; you've found your self-respect.

Dear Pat,

I really honestly believe that I don't need friends. I have God. I don't need anyone else. Comments?

A Christian Vulcan

Dear Saint Spock,

Yes, I have a comment from the Starship *Eternity*: "This is My commandment, that you love one another, just as I have loved you. Greater love has no one than this, that one lay down his life for his friends" (John 15:12–13).

Jesus Christ really honestly believes that you do need friends. He is God, and He thinks you need someone else, even though a friend may have hurt you in the past. If you don't believe Him, you've got a theological problem. If you believe Him but are afraid to reach out to others, you've got a faith problem. If you believe Him but don't know how to be a friend, you've got a social problem. If you believe Him but refuse to be a friend, you'll be alone with your problems for the rest of your life. I don't believe you really honestly want that.

Identify the problem. You were created to obey Him and enjoy His creation. That includes people. Admit your need and admit that you have ears.

Dear Pat,

Is popularity good or bad?

Webster, Jr.

Dear Webs,

Popularity can seem good:

If you're a girl who's lost thirty pounds, gotten rid of her braces, permed her hair, and tanned all summer. You could be very popular in September.

If you've just caught a pass for the winning touchdown with no time left on the clock and that gives your school the league championship, then you're popular.

If you've just convinced your teacher to hold off giving a test until after the weekend, then "popularity" is your middle name.

If you're the kind of person who makes friends with everyone and never does anything to upset their feelings, then you'd be called "popular."

So is popularity good? Not necessarily. It makes you feel good for a while, but it can be a trap, too.

If your goal is to be popular, then you're not thinking of others first. If you want others to really like you, it could be easy for you to worry about their approval rather than God's holiness. I'd like to see you concentrate on being truthful and sensitive to Him and respond to others out of that obedience. You may not always be popular, but you'll be faithful, and that's very popular with God.

Dear Pat,

The guy I'm dating is my best friend's former boyfriend. She's no longer my best friend. In fact, she won't even talk to me. How can we be friends again?

Really Hurt

Dear RH,

Sit down with your best friend and ask her for the definition of friendship. Do real friends always agree? Do real friends ever get upset with each other? Do real friends ever make mistakes for which they're sorry later? Read Prov. 17:17 together.

She'll probably tell you that a real friend doesn't go out with the guy she used to date! Then you have some choices. Here are your options:

1. "You're right. I made a mistake. I didn't realize you still liked him. Dating him isn't worth our friendship. I'll stop seeing him because I know it's hurting you."

2. "You had your chance with this guy. It didn't work out. You're free to see other people, and so's he. He's chosen to spend time with me. I don't want to lose our friendship over this, but I have the right to date him."

3. "What is it that really angers you? Is it that you want him back? Is it that he seems to be choosing me over you? Is it that you don't think any of your friends should ever date any of your old boyfriends? What?"

The two of you need to get together and talk. If she won't, then put your thoughts in a letter. A good friend is hard to find. I'd like to see you remain friends, but you're going to have to face this issue together. That's the way friends are.

> Dear Pat,
>
> What really goes on at slumber parties?
>
> A Curious Guy

Dear CG,

Are you ready to hear some of the most unbelievable stuff in your life? Get ready.

They eat like horses When girls get together, they shovel it down. Pizza . . . potato chips . . . doughnuts. The food's gone. Then they lie around on the floor like beached whales, moaning. "Oh, I've eaten too much" . . . "This is going to wreck my diet" . . . "I'm never eating again." Then someone says the magic word: "Chocolate"!

Jane Fonda eat your heart out After all that food, it's time for exercise. They head for the outdoors and toilet paper everything: trees, pets, people, houses, cars, and half of the Western world.

Going to the bathroom A girl never goes to the bathroom at slumber parties. The moment she leaves the room, all the other girls start talking about her! "She's so gross!" "Why'd you invite her?" "Did you see what she's wearing?" "I'm not going outside with her!" etc. Girls would rather wait twelve hours and explode than turn their backs on some of their friends.

Exciting games The favorite game of many girls is called Truth or Dare! The contestant gets to answer a question posed by the rest of the herd. She has to tell the truth, regardless of how embarrassing the truth can be. For example: "Okay, you were with Brad on Friday night. How far did you . . ."

The victim sits there with buckets of sweat pouring off her as the rest of the girls move in like vultures. If you don't answer the question, then you take the dare. She might put on bright boxer shorts and run up and down the street screaming, "I think Boy George is a fox!" rather than answer the question.

Some things never change The thing that girls like to do most at slumber parties is talk about guys. When girls talk about guys they get very blunt! "What does he kiss like?" . . . "Niagara Falls!" "Is his breath really bad?" . . . "Well, it smells like a camel died in his mouth!" "After kissing him, what would his nickname be?" . . . "Tonsil Mouth! Gross!"

I think that most girls learn to kiss at slumber parties. I'm told they tape pictures of their favorite television and movie stars on little pillows and then practice by smashing their faces into the pillows. With their eyes closed, of course. So if you see a few rumpled little pillows, you know they've been to a slumber party.

Dear Pat,

I'm getting ready to graduate from high school, but I'm sad because I'm going to lose a lot of my friends. Help?!

The Goodbye Girl

Dear Gigi,

No problem. I have three suggestions guaranteed to help you keep your friends a little longer.

Flunk This gives you another year together. Of course, your friends would have to cooperate and flunk, too. This way you'd find out who your real friends are!

Buy a college Once you get your own university, make it tuition-free so all your friends can go there. If you don't have the ready cash, you could have a bake sale or something.

Bump your head Hard to let go of those emotions? Amnesia works every time. No memory—no moping! Go find a wall and start your new life with a smile!

Or you could thank God for His timing. "There is an appointed time for everything. And there is a time for every event under heaven. . . . A time to embrace, and a time to shun embracing" (Eccles. 3:1, 5).

God gave you the perfect friends for your life in high school. As I write this, He's already preparing your new friends to be just what you need for the next four years.

Dear Pat,

I have a friend who's always
negative. No matter what I say,
he's always critical. Is there
anything I can do?

Worn Out

Dear WO,

Try this: Get a Polaroid camera and take a
beautiful picture (a sunset or something), peel off
the negative, and hand it to your friend. Show him
your beautiful picture and compare it to his negative. Ask him which he would rather have to carry
around with him. If he says, "The negative," then
you're in trouble.

If he prefers the beautiful picture, explain that
you prefer to look at the bright side most of the time,
too. Then tell him how his negativeness sometimes
frustrates you. Ask him if he has noticed how negative he tends to be. He may not be aware of it. He
may think it's normal to be negative. He may have
a rough family life.

Jesus had a disciple who tended to be negative. His name was Thomas. We have three stories
about Thomas in the Scriptures. In every case he
had a negative comment toward the situation. But
there's a deeper side to Thomas than just his bad
mood; he cared too much about things. Because
he wanted everything and everyone to be perfect,
Thomas used his negativism as a defense to hide his
real emotions. He loved Jesus so much that he never
wanted Jesus to leave him.

Your friend may be emotionally sensitive. He may love too much. How would he cover that up? Perhaps by being negative. It's always easier to act like you don't care than to admit that you care too much.

Thomas was negative because he loved so deeply that he was afraid of being left out. Inside he wanted someone to care very much, and so does your friend.

Dear Pat,

How do I tell someone he's phony?

Wanting to Be Honest

Dear Wanda,

The best way to tell someone he or she is phony is to prepare yourself first.

Admit that you're phony once in a while This will help you be patient and understanding when you go to talk to your friend. Remember that you would want someone to be gentle with you when you're not perfect.

Realize phoniness is a front for something else Don't attack the person; confront the problem. The real problem with phoniness is fear. We are afraid to be ourselves because we don't want to be rejected. So we try to be someone we're not. Read Eph. 4:15 and confront the heart of the fear issue. Until fear is dealt with, the phoniness will never go away.

Fearful people need to be encouraged Jesus recognized this with Peter, one of the biggest phonies in the Bible. His approach to Peter was, "Peter, I know you're always trying to impress me, but you don't have to. Just be yourself and trust me with your fears." Peter learned to fail, and the phoniness disappeared.

Your friend needs a real friend If you can tell this person, "Look, I'm your friend. Even if you aren't always honest, I'm still your friend. I won't be phony with you, and I don't want you to be phony with me." Then I think you can get your message across. Don't condemn; be encouraging.

Dear Pat,

I've got a good friend who's slowly killing himself. It involves drugs and sex. I don't know what to do! Can you tell me how to help?

No Place to Go

Dear NOP,

There are some things you can do. If you're a good friend, you'll do them! Here are some steps.

Gather other friends for support Don't try to tackle this alone. Get some mutual friends together who are trustworthy and mature. Talk through the problem your friend has, as well as possible solutions. Be very careful to do this prayerfully and not as gossip.

Commit your friend to prayer As a group, you need to begin praying for your friend every day before you even approach him. Ask God for wisdom, strength, and gentleness as you get ready for the talk you need to have.

Choose a solution for the problem You know the problem, and you know your friend. I want you to find a Christian adult to consult with on what solution would be appropriate for this particular situation.

Confront your friend Give your friend two choices. Tell him to seek help or you're going to tell his parents to stop this slow version of suicide. Tell your friend this isn't easy for all of you to do, but as a friend you want to do whatever is possible to help. Expect him to be angry and to say things out of anger that he may not really mean. Stay close to him and watch carefully. He may try one desperate act to really hurt himself out of shame.

His parents may need to know There are some cases in which the parents should be informed. I'll trust you to consider this according to the situation. You're dealing with rebuilding a life and minimizing the damage.

Dear Pat,

I have a friend who keeps talking about suicide. What can I do?

Pro Life

Dear Pro,

You can do several things:

Tell your friend how important he (or she) is Your friend isn't only special to God but to you, too. People who seriously consider suicide have forgotten how special they are.

Ask him to tell you about his depression Suicide isn't the problem, it's a method to end the problem. Be a listener and gain the confidence of your friend. Get him to talk about what's really bothering him. Don't give advice, just listen.

Take him to a counselor You aren't equipped to counsel your friend when it comes to suicidal tendencies. Offer to go with your friend to a Christian psychologist. Most people who consider suicide, feel alone. You need to be with him to the best of your ability. But get your friend some help. It's very important.

Don't take responsibility for the results You can only do so much. You can't control another person's life. If your friend kills himself, that's his decision. Don't blame yourself. You did what you could. If he recovers and goes on to lead a great life, don't take the credit. He made that decision, too. You're a friend, a friend who wants him to live. Keep telling him that.

Dear Pat,

This may sound really stupid, but how do I make friends?

A Little Lonely

Dear Allie,

It's not a stupid question. In fact, it's one of the most common questions I ever hear. Here are some ideas.

Be friendly with everyone you meet There's so much negativism in the world that it's refreshing to meet someone who smiles and is pleasant. The first time a person meets you creates an impression he or she won't forget. Give them a smile to remember.

Ask them questions "Have you lived here most of your life?" or "What's fun to do in this town?" will start to give you an idea of the kind of person he or she is. By asking about interests, you can find out if you have anything in common. That's where friendships begin. But you start by asking questions. Don't wait for the other person to do it.

Don't talk negatively about others You're meeting people for the first time. Trust is very important here. They may make fun of their friends. But if you do the same to win their respect, it could backfire on you later. Let them gossip and stay out of it. It's the best way to lose friends, not make them.

Be yourself Don't try to impress them and don't pretend to be someone you're not. Either they'll accept you or they won't. It's better to be rejected than to be a phony. You can always make new friends.

Dear Pat,

My friends gossip a lot! When I'm
around them, I find it easy to do
the same thing. Can you help?

Motor Mouth

Dear Mi Mi,

Here's a great proverb:

When there are many words, transgression is
    unavoidable,
But he who restrains his lips is wise.
The tongue of the righteous is *as* choice silver,
The heart of the wicked is *worth* little.

(Prov. 10:19–20)

The verses before and after are also excellent.

Let's face it: we gossip because it makes us look
better. By tearing someone down, we see their faults
and ignore our own. The next time you are tempted
to rip into someone, remember:

Would Jesus Christ talk like that about you?
Would He always be encouraging about you
    to others whenever your name came up?
Do you really feel condemning toward that
    person? Are you being that way to get the
    approval of your friends?
Do you want to use your gift of speech to lift up
    Jesus Christ or as a tool to bring someone else
    down?

It's time to fine tune your motor, Mi Mi.

Dear Pat,

I've got two really good friends,
but whenever the three of us are
together, we can't get along! Why?

Three's a Crowd

Dear Threedie Bird,

Of course, the three of you don't get along!
That's the way it usually works! Can you say "jealousy"? Let me get specific.

When you and one of your good friends are
together, you have a bond, which means that you
share things that involve just the two of you. This is
pretty special stuff. You look at each other as if to
say, "Hey, we're really close; this is private between
us. No one else could possibly understand what we
feel at this moment." Does that sound familiar?

So what happens when a third person comes
into that special relationship? Maybe nothing happens, but the chances are good that one or both of
you will be a little confused as to how much you
want this other person to be involved in your special
relationship.

You may feel guilty because this third person
is a good friend and yet a stranger to the feelings
you experience with your other friend. As you try
to make everyone happy, you find that one of you
usually gets hurt.

The solution is simpler than you think. Enjoy
special bonds with several friends on different
emotional levels. There's no rule that says you have
to relate to just one best friend. Don't limit yourself
or put that kind of pressure on others.

Dear Pat,

I've got a friend with a bad hygiene habit. Should I tell him? How do I do it?

Gassed Out

Dear Gasty,

I had a friend like that once. You could always smell him coming. He rarely took showers and wore the same clothes all the time.

One day he came to class with an infected zit. It was green! It looked like Kermit the Frog had died on his chin! We finally said, "Jerry, do something with that zit. It's gross!"

So, a couple of days later he came to class with a huge Band-aid on his chin. We asked him about the zit. He smiled and said, "I got it this morning with a knitting needle." Took me a half bottle of Windex to clean off my mirror!" We died laughing. Jerry had made pondscum on his face an art form!

What should you say to your friend? Try this: "You have a lot of great qualities, and I know that you respect yourself. Because you do, I'd like to give you a few constructive suggestions that might improve your appearance. Are you interested?"

Be polite and respectful. Emphasize the positive. Your friend will not only benefit from it, but you'll learn to be a better friend.

Dear Pat,

Why are there cliques?

Tired of the Social Game

Dear Tired,

There are cliques because groups who have something in common like to hang out together. There are various names for them, but you may recognize some of the more common groups: jocks, druggies, goat ropers (cowboys), greasers, punks, student council smacks, surfers, smokers, and the Jesus freaks.

Jesus saw cliques in His day: Sadducees, Pharisees, Romans, militant Jews, Lepers, and disciples.

There's nothing wrong with a bunch of people who have similar interests spending time together. But if you think your group is better than another group, then you have problems. We don't judge individuals by their group, and we don't judge groups by our differences.

Paul writes, "For though I am free from all *men,* I have made myself a slave to all, that I might win the more" (1 Cor. 9:19). He goes on to say that he became as a Jew to the Jews; to those under the Law or without the Law, he would relate to them; to the weak, he became weak: "I have become all things to all men (cliques), that I may by all means save some" (1 Cor. 9:22b).

The issue is not playing the game for selfish popularity but relating to all types for an unselfish ministry.

Dear Pat,

I always hear the term "peer pressure," but I'm not exactly sure what it means?

Keep It Simple

Dear Simon,

Peer pressure can be broken down this way: peer = a friend or classmate about your age; pressure = strong influence that affects you.

Let's say you go to a party. You don't plan on drinking anything stronger than milk. Once you get there, you find a bunch of your friends are drinking vodka with their cookies. They say, "Aren't you gonna get drunk with us? You know you want to! Let's throw up together!" So you agree that this sounds like a lot of fun, and you trade in your 2 percent for the hard stuff. You get home bombed out of your ever-lovin' mind.

Your parents are waiting up for you as you stagger into the house. "You're drunk!" they scream. "Why did you get drunk?!" You are no longer having fun. Some teenagers will think quickly and say, "My friends made me do it! It was . . . uh . . . peer pressure!" This makes mom and dad feel a little better, because it allows them to blame other parents' kids for the fact that their own child has the backbone of a marshmallow.

Peer pressure has allowed people to get away with things for years. It's still very popular today.

The truth? You did it because you wanted to do it. Remember: people always do what they want to do! I will respect you, Simon, if you take the heat for your own decisions. Right or wrong, don't pass the buck.

```
Dear Pat,

My best friend and I aren't
speaking. It's been this way
for a week. Any ideas?

                         Dug In
```

Dear Dug,

This is a tough one. There's so much emotion
here that you both have to be willing to compromise
a bit. Try these steps.

Admit your sin in the problem (Matt. 7:3-5) In
any argument, both parties have a responsibility to
look at what they've done wrong. Before you go
any further, accept your mistakes first. Otherwise,
you'll be blaming your friend for a long, long time.

Ask God to forgive you (Ps. 51:1-4) Settle your
issue with your Heavenly Father before you go to
anyone else. This is between you and Him.

Pray for your best friend (Eph. 4:31-32) Even
though you're not speaking, you're still best friends.
Thank God every time you think of your friend and
lift him or her up in prayer no matter how you feel.

Identify the real hurt (Heb. 12:1) What really
bothers you about this argument? Was it something
that was said? A breakdown in trust? An action
taken that hurt you? You and your friend may have
totally different versions of the problem.

Take the first step (Heb. 12:14) God has called
us as Christians to live at peace with our Christian
brothers and sisters. Go in gentleness and don't look
for blame. It may go better than you think.

Dear Pat,

How come some people never have a best friend? Like me?

Wishing for One

Dear Wishy,

Let's look at some of the positive reasons why you don't need a best friend.

It is healthier to have several good friends When just two people are close, there's a tendency to look at life from a narrow perspective. When you open yourself up to others, you get a lot of great ideas which get you out of the tunnel and help you see the world in a healthier sense.

You avoid jealousy Trying to always be close to just one person can make us uptight if someone else enters the picture. We tend to resent the new person because we never had to share our best friend with anyone before. With several friends, there's less jealousy.

You have more options What if your best friend doesn't want to do what you want to do on a Friday night? If you go, he or she is left alone at home. With several good friends, you have a variety of things to do and no guilt.

It will develop your personality You have many sides. Many friends will deepen those many qualities. You'll be multidimensional. You'll be a neapolitan kind of ice-cream kid.

Some people have best friends. It works for them. But be happy with the many friends God has given you.

Dear Pat,

I have a friend who's not real popular at school. I mean, he's a nerd, in a way. But I really like him, and everyone always asks me why. What do I tell them?

The Defender

Dear Deffy,

Ask them some questions about your friend. First, ask them why this person bothers them so much. Ask them to be specific. Is it his breath? His body odor? The shape of his glasses? His style of clothing? If they say, "He's just a loser" (or something similar), then you ask them, "Does any person deserve the kind of criticism and comments that you're making?" If they say yes he does, then ask them what terrible thing has made him the butt of all their jokes.

Keep putting the pressure on your critical friends to say what they really mean. Eventually they're going to tell the truth. Namely, "We simply think we're better than him." When they say that, you have a choice. Do you really want to hang around with people who aren't sensitive to those who lack certain social graces? Remember: "Do nothing from selfishness or empty conceit, but with humility of mind let each of you regard one another as more important than himself" (Phil. 2:3).

Dear Pat,

My parents don't like my friends.
I think they're being unfair. How
do I convince them that my friends
aren't all that bad?

The Verdict Is Guilty

Dear Verdi,

My parents didn't like my friends either. Of course, they had some good reasons. My wonderful friends used to hide my dad's books in the refrigerator. He'd go to get ice cream and see his favorite novel shivering behind the Eskimo Pies!

Then there was the time they asked to borrow his new truck for a few hours to help me land a job in a neighboring town. Instead we drove eight hundred miles to Los Angeles and back. We came within three inches of totalling it on the Santa Monica Freeway.

Then there was the night we played hide and seek with the police. My friends hid, and I got seeked. And caught! My dad was real thrilled about that one.

I always defended my friends. Why? Because I hung around with them. They weren't all that bad. We were just a little crazy. We thought everyone enjoyed riding on the luggage rack on top of a car at forty miles an hour.

Looking back, my parents were right. They shouldn't have trusted me or my friends. I wouldn't admit that then. I acknowledge it now. If your friends are really trustworthy, Verdi, your parents will eventually see it. Until they do, be real honest with yourself and your actions. Ask yourself if you're proving your trust when you're with your friends.

> Dear Pat,
>
> What are the qualities of a good friend?
>
> > Looking to Trust

Dear Trust,

I think there are five qualities that make a great friend.

Honesty I've never seen a good friendship work without this quality. I've seen a lot of friendships end when someone lies. It's the backbone of any relationship.

Loyalty People aren't perfect. Friends will make mistakes. The test of a true friendship is how we hang in there when one of our friends makes a mistake.

Consistency It's important to be able to count on each other, especially if things get tense all around you. There needs to be a pattern of relating that you can build on together.

Common interests You can have opposite personalities, but you'd better have things you like to do in common. If those common interests change, your friendship will probably fade.

Chemistry There's something between you two that makes you want to be close to that person. You really "click." That's always evident between best friends.

Dear Pat,

I have a friend who's not a Christian. My youth pastor told me to pray for him. That sounds nice, but does it really do anything?

Doubting Thomas

Dear Thomas,

Whether your friend is a guy or girl, prayer *does* work! Let me tell you something incredible that happened to me before I gave my heart to Jesus Christ.

I decided to pay a surprise visit to a very good friend who lived in Los Angeles. It was about a five-hour drive from my home to his house, and I arrived quite late, some time after midnight. The door wasn't locked, so I walked right in. He was in the living room. When he saw me, his face looked like he had seen a ghost. I couldn't understand why he was so surprised. It had only been two years since we last saw each other. He had no idea I was coming, but it wasn't that big of a deal! I found out the truth the following year.

Soon after I became a Christian, I wrote Darryl a letter and told him about my new faith. I encouraged him to give his life to Jesus Christ, too. That's when I realized the power of God through prayer.

Darryl told me that one night he had been feeling guilty about never sharing his Christian faith with me. He knew I was going to hell unless I embraced the grace of God. At that moment, God convicted him to get down on his knees and pray for me. He was doing that when I walked into his living room that night. Then and there he knew I was going to become a Christian someday. A year later, I did just that. So you tell me, do you think prayer works on your friends?

Dear Pat,

I'm not getting along with certain friends, and I think I'm expecting too much. Are there different levels of friendship?

Charting the Hits

Dear Chart,

Yes, as a matter of fact, there are levels of friendship. I'll attempt to explain them in order of intimacy.

Friend for life Less than a handful of people—sometimes just one—will be a friend for the rest of your life. I'm not talking about people you know, I'm talking about a real friend. If you have one for life, you're really fortunate.

Best friend for now Getting through high school requires some understanding and a friend to run with through thick and thin. You'll store up memories like chipmunks save acorns. You'll look through your yearbook twenty years from now and smile at the page of your "best friend," the one you've only seen three times since then.

Friend in a crisis I remember a party one night when my good friend, John Rasmussen, was told by a girl that she liked him more than her boyfriend, who was standing right there. Ras and I left the party. We drove around and talked until three o'clock in the morning. A policeman pulled us over, and I calmly explained that Ras and I just needed time to talk. I haven't seen Ras in fifteen years, but we were very close that night.

A teammate for a season This isn't limited to just sports. It could also be a debate partner, a campaign helper, a yearbook coeditor, or a homecoming coorganizer. It could even be a homeroom pal—just for the semester. When the project, the season, or the semester is over, so is the chemistry between you and your short-term "best friend." Say good-bye.

The painful friend There'll be people you'll have to work with, like student council or sports or band or the school newspaper, and you don't really like them. But they're good for you because they cause you to work hard at being honest or be a better person to keep up with their criticism. There are times when you want to kill them, but someday you'll look back and say, "I'm glad I had that person on my back. He (or she) caused me to improve as a human being!" But for now, yuk!

The fair-weather friend When things are going well, they're your friends. But when the weather gets "stormy," they'll leave you in a minute. These people aren't your real friends. They're users.

The party animal They seem like great friends until you try to be responsible. Then they drift away to find people who just want to have fun. You can't trust these folks either.

We aren't expected to be close friends with everyone. We aren't supposed to trust or confide in everyone either. Just know who your real friends are and for how long.

Dear Pat

What's the greatest thing someone
can do for his friends?

The Lover

Dear Lover,

The greatest thing you can do is give your life
for them. Since God will probably never ask you to
do that, the next best thing is to tell them how Jesus
gave His life for them.

My best friend in high school introduced me to
drinking, drugs, and partying. He and I used to
hitchhike down to Los Angeles. Once we lived there
for most of a summer, during which we almost got
killed about three times.

Of all my memories, the one I'll never forget is
September 3, 1969. That's when he sat me down at
my dining room table and said, "Pat, can I talk to
you about Jesus Christ?" I was shocked.

Before I could say, "No thanks," he pulled out
a four spiritual laws booklet and started reading.
Twenty minutes later, I bowed my head and asked
Jesus Christ to come into my life with my best friend
sitting there next to me. I'll always thank God for
Mike Burke.

How I long for you to come to Christ. My
heart is heavy within me and I grieve bitterly
day and night because of you. Christ knows
and the Holy Spirit knows that it is no mere
pretense when I say that I would be willing to
be forever damned if that would save you.

(Rom. 9:1b-3, LB)

I hope you can be that kind of friend to someone.

- 59 -

High School

Things guaranteed to drive you crazy

Dear Pat,

As a Christian, what are some ways I can take a stand for Jesus Christ on my high-school campus?

Ready for Ignition

Dear Read,

It's surprising how few Christians ask me that question. It's much easier to fit in quietly with everybody else. Looking back over the years, I can think of some high-school students who wanted to be different and who taught me the real faith of being a man or woman of God under pressure.

See your campus as a mission field A young lady and her brother in southern California transferred from their Christian school to a public school because they wanted the challenge of reaching as many unbelievers as they could for Jesus Christ. They believed Matt. 9:36–38: "And seeing the multitudes, He felt compassion for them, because they were distressed and downcast like sheep without a shepherd. Then He said to His disciples, 'The harvest is plentiful, but the workers are few. Therefore beseech the Lord of the harvest to send out workers into His harvest.'"

Okay, harvesters, here are some ways you can help your friends hear more about the Word of God.

Claim a specific group for Jesus Christ Rather than take on the whole school, focus on a group with whom you feel most comfortable. One senior decided his baseball team needed Christ. One of the pitchers who led him to Christ began to pray that his vision for the team could come true. Within three weeks, four of the guys had accepted Christ and three other players rededicated their lives! If it can happen to a baseball team, it can happen to the school band, the student council, the cheerleaders, or even the shop class.

Creative speaking If you have to give a speech and be nervous anyway, why don't you give the glory to God? Students in your class might be interested in the person of Jesus Christ and how He differs from other famous people of history. You could explain the End Times as predicted by the Bible or describe the remarkable Old Testament prophecies coming true—all 331 of them! Well, you may want to keep it down to a few of the major ones for the sake of time. Add a little humor, and you might be surprised how little your friends know about God. Their salvation is more important than your grade on one speech. The same is true for term papers or essays written for class assignments.

Newspaper staff As a columnist, you can let people know how superficial their high-school world is without God. As a reporter, you can do special features on what Christians are doing on campus. As an editor, you can write editorials on real solutions to the problems in this world. After all, it's a free country; you can express your opinion on anything you want.

Small-group Bible study Why wait for people to come to your church? Start gathering other Christians where the action is—on your campus! You could meet before school, at lunch, or during a free period. There's nothing illegal about this as long as you're not disrupting class or forcing someone else to listen. As a small group of Christians, you can begin to pray for your school. You can even invite friends who normally wouldn't go near a church to join your group.

Evangelistic Bible club Two girls in a junior high school in Sacramento asked to use a room once a week after school, and they got it! Thirty-seven students showed up for the first meeting. That's more than you should expect, but whatever God gives you is a great start. Figure out some goals for your Bible club just like you would with any other club. Make sure that its main purpose is to share the Gospel with unbelievers, otherwise it'll die out.

Creative use of your youth leader Most youth pastors don't spend time on the high-school campus. They're too busy planning clever activities to keep Christians coming to church. Don't let your youth minister get by that easily. Put him or her to work at your school. Ideas?

> chaplain for a sports team
> coordinator, athletic or scholastic prayer break-
>   fasts
> classroom speaker (you might even get extra
>   credit!)
> volunteer coach for sports or speech team
>   part-time counselor at school (My students
>   helped me get an office at two different
>   schools.)

Remember: the harvest is there. Either we reap it or Satan will. These are your friends. Their eternal life is important!

> Dear Pat,
>
> What were the hardest courses in your high school days?
>
> > Nostalgic

Dear Nostaldamus,

The toughest classes? That's easy.

Algebra To this day I have a hard time understanding why $x = y^2$ is important to anyone besides a rocket scientist. It can't make you money. It can't cook your burger in less than thirty seconds. You can't wear it. It doesn't smell as good as English Leather. It was in that class that I got my first and only sinus infection. I was lucky I never took Algebra II.

Latin If I ever see *amo, amas, amat* again in my lifetime, I will gag on a towel. Julius Caesar deserved to die.

Typing Most people hit the keys; I found the holes. They didn't give me a grade, they bought me Band-aids!

Chemistry The only reason I took chemistry was to figure out how to build a bomb to blow up that stupid element chart that mocked me every morning with initials. Mg. Yuk! Sorry. I got carried away.

Driver's education I wanted my license; I *didn't* want to see the films that made Freddy Krueger look like an Eagle Scout. I saw more blood in six weeks than Dracula sipped in seventeen movies! These movies had great titles: *Blood Alley, The Last Prom, Red Asphalt,* and *When the Laughter Died.* As I watched one gory scene after another, one thought kept running through my mind: "How *did* these people pass driving tests?" They made a six-lane highway look like the last hole on a miniature golf course. Hey folks, stay on the road. It's not that tough. It's *paved!*

Spanish It would have helped if they had (1) let us ask questions in English, and (2) taught our teacher Spanish.

English lit I know *Beowulf* is a classic, and I know Shakespeare is a genius. Now can I get on with my life? Thouest pleasest? Thankest youest! Ughest!

Biology The all-time downer class. If it grows, study it. If it reacts, explain it. If it's green, identify it. If it croaks, dissect it. If it keeps on croaking, you haven't dissected it enough! I'll never forget that lab smell as long as I live. My dad'll never forget my grade either!

Dear CO,

The following attributes make quality teachers:

They treat students with respect If you see a teacher talking down to students or acting like you guys are a pain (or a problem), then that instructor has violated the basic rule of motivation: Raise the level of your audience! A good teacher sees a student as being as good as he or she is.

They know their stuff One of the biggest complaints from students is the teacher who "doesn't know what he's talking about." Good teachers know their subject matter in-depth. If they *don't* know something, they're humble enough to admit it.

They don't just teach—they communicate Communication is not what you say; it's what the other person hears! A lot of teachers believe they're teaching, but they're not. They're disseminating information. If you don't know what "disseminating information" means, then I've just proven my point.

They don't major on the minors Good teachers understand the individual needs of their students. They don't waste time harping on something that's not going to improve the quality of that person's life. They know what issues are important and what issues aren't.

They're professional Your teachers aren't your parents or your buddies; they're paid to do a good job. That means they're supposed to prepare you for that particular subject or discipline. A good teacher doesn't let emotions or problems hamper that goal.

Dear Pat,

I want to try out for cheerleading. What are some things I can do to get ready?

Suzie Spirit

Dear Suzie,

I'm glad you asked me for help. Follow these instructions carefully.

Smile wherever you go I don't mean smile most of the time; I want you to smile *all* of the time! If someone trips and breaks a leg—*smile!* If someone chokes on food—*smile!* If someone's pet dies—*smile!* This way you can learn to make the student body feel good when your team is losing 63–0.

Pretend you're not going to be a cheerleader After the tryouts, it's always great to say, "I *know* they won't pick me! I know they'll pick **you!**" etc. This way you're protected no matter what happens! If they pick your friend, then you were right. If they pick you, then you were humble. Either way, you're covered.

Wear a paper bag over your head A very important rule for most cheerleaders is that you must never know what is going on around you. If your team is driving for a touchdown, you must still be able to cheer something opposite like, "Dee-fense!" This way you're the main part of the game—not the players!

Learn to clap your hands You have to clap at everything. When you hear homeroom announcements—*clap!* When someone burps in class—*clap!* When the other team scores—*clap!* This will show lots of spirit and enthusiasm. You don't have to be a nuclear scientist; you just need to keep moving. Good luck!

- 69 -

Dear Pat,

Can I succeed in life without a
high-school degree?

Dropping Out

Dear Dropo,

Sure! Life without a high-school diploma is a lot
like:

- Throwing a pass on fourth-and-long from your
  own two-yard line with six seconds on the
  game clock and needing a touchdown to
  win . . .
- Going up to the best-looking girl in the school
  and asking her to the prom without using de-
  odorant or brushing your teeth for a week . . .
- Asking your dad for the car keys after you've
  just posted bail for robbing a bank . . .
- Trying to make friends with the drug crowd
  after they've found out you work for the Jus-
  tice Department . . .

Anything is possible, but the percentages are
not on your side. The more education you get, the
better chance you have of society opening doors
for you.

Getting a diploma says something about your
character, your value system, your determination,
and your desire to achieve. Dropping out says something about those things, too—whether you like it
or not.

We're not judged by what we feel capable of
doing; we're judged by what we've already done.
Shorten your odds; get your degree.

Dear Pat,

What are high schools like in California?

A Midwest Kind of Guy

Dear Middie,

High schools in California are just average. Every girl is blonde and tan, without an ounce of fat anywhere on her body! All they eat is Special K. They have perfect, white teeth, and they're always having fun at the beach, which is where the classes are held.

The teachers don't give homework because there aren't any books. Instead, they issue you towels, surfboards, sun tan lotion, and a gift certificate for unlimited pizza! It's like no where else.

There are some tough classes, though. Here's a sample schedule:

1st period: dynamics of sleeping in
2nd period: basics of credit-card shopping
3rd period: mall science (field trip)
4th period: lunch
5th period: lunch
6th period: advanced beach volleyball
7th period: pictorial history of bathing suits
8th period: literature of twentieth-century
    movies

I wouldn't recommend transferring out here; it's a pretty rigorous academic discipline. It's not for everybody. Besides, there's no snow here, and they don't have autumn. I think you're much better off where you are . . . really . . . I'm serious . . . you'd miss wearing six layers of clothing . . . trust me . . .

Dear Pat,

I was thinking about joining a club on campus. Which one do you recommend?

Indecisive

Dear Indy,

Here's a quick guide to clubs on campus with my ridiculous comments added:

Chess club

A bunch of people who like to stare at things that hardly ever move. Rumor has it that they fall asleep or even die during games.

Any foreign-language club

Never get excited about a foreign language whose country has never seen a Pizza Hut. You'll just be disappointed.

Typing club

No way—the students are too keyed up!

Drama club

This is a place where you can wear different faces and still keep your friends.

Speech club

For people who like to talk and are convinced that others really want to listen.

Student council

This is not a club; this is a "privilege." If you don't believe me, then watch the way some of them act.

Pep club

They eat a lot of bran.

Dear Pat,

Why do teachers give so much homework? Geez!

Overloaded

Dear Oville,

There are several reasons why there is so much homework floating around:

Teachers tend to be content-oriented This isn't good news for you. Most instructors think that education is facts and figures. So that means a lot of reading and researching and very little interpretation of it. That philosophy makes for a long evening for you and your friends, pal.

Teaching: a job—not an adventure You may have a lot of exciting things you'd like to do in an average day. But teachers are paid to focus on one aspect of your life—your education. When they think about your evening or your weekend, they don't think about your dating life or the parties you want to attend. They do think about making certain you remember stuff from class.

Homework says a lot about you It's not whether the chemistry chart or the Latin derivatives are something you'll use when you're forty years old, but how you respond to an assignment is a clue to your character. Success isn't what you learn, it's your desire to learn it and use it for a purpose.

To this day, I don't remember anything about my homework, but I did learn a lot about deadlines and responsibility. So finish that paper and don't tell your teacher that your *ficuna* ate it.

```
Dear Pat,

My friends all want me to run for
office, but I'm afraid I might
lose. What should I do?

                          Undeclared
```

Dear Undy,

It boils down to what is most important to you.
I ran for president once in a mock convention, and I
lost. I lost because some people got together and
threw all their votes to the other guy who beat me
on the fourth ballot. I'll never forget the feeling I
had as I walked out of the gym that day. I didn't
feel bad, and I wasn't angry. I had given it my best
shot, and I'd come up short. It was okay to lose an
election. I still had a lot left over.

I still had my friends, I still had my self-respect,
and I still had my health. I still had my sense of humor, and I had my family. I still had my life. It was
nothing more than an election.

You're going to win and lose all your life. That's
something you do, not someone you are. If you try
something and "fail," you've only added an experience to your life—not marked your soul for eternity.

I want to encourage you to ask God for wisdom
and courage as you go after those experiences. It's
not whether you run for office or not. It's not whether
you win or lose. It's whether you are going to thank
Him for the result. Read 2 Tim. 1:9.

Dear Pat,

Why do people put down cafeteria food? I enjoy it.

Shovel Man

Dear Shovel,

I enjoyed cafeteria food, too. Of course, when I was in high school, they cooked it by candlelight. In fact, a lot of it tasted like candle wax. There were some real special meals.

Trans-World tostada airlines Also known as "tacos," they made sure you got to class on time. In fact, you flew out that door! If anyone had lit a match in the cafeteria that day, we'd have been the sequel to Sodom and Gomorrah!

Raiders of the lost recipe Remember Indiana Jones? Remember the snakes? Slimy, gooshy, and . . . moving. That reminded me of something I ate at least once a week in my cafeteria. I think they called it spaghetti. It would have killed the snakes!

Bill Cosby, eat your heart out The two desserts they always served were Jell-o with a pulled muscle and pudding that tasted like meat loaf out of a blender. I always laugh when I see the cute commercials Bill Cosby does for Jell-o; if he'd have eaten in our cafeteria, he'd be selling stomach pumps.

So go ahead and eat. Make my day.

Dear Pat,

I'm always getting into trouble in school. Did you ever get kicked out of class?

The Rebel

Dear Robert E. Lee, Jr.,

Did I ever get kicked out of class? Well, yes and no . . .

I got bored easily in school. So whenever the teacher made a comment, I was always there to improve on it. This was my mission in life. I was destined to bring chaos to normal routines.

One day, I had the class cracking up, and my government teacher decided to make a move on me and my games. He instructed two of the students to move my desk outside the classroom so that I could attend class from a distance. I could hear him, but no one could hear me. This happened more than once, so it became familiar to the entire class to learn all about current events while I sat outside dodging birds who had just lunched at a chili stand.

Looking back at my behavior, I have to admit that I was pretty selfish and very insecure to bring all that attention to myself. It wasn't fair to my teacher, and it wasn't fair to the rest of the class. I was looking to release a lot of tension inside. I needed counseling.

And it wasn't fair to the birds; they should have used the public restrooms like everyone else.

Dear Pat,

Does every high school really have at least one teacher who looks like a walrus?

Wally Watcher

Dear Wally,

Yes, it's definitely true. This isn't limited to sex, either. Walruses especially enjoy teaching.

There are some other teacher types that can be found at every high school in America:

Freddy, the shop hacker *Nightmare on Elm Street* really began in shop class. There's usually a teacher with a nervous twitch and a bad haircut. He wears an apron, and he loves to cut! Think about it. He's out there.

The underground librarian Where does she come from? Where does she go at night? She moves through the library, and you never see her until it's too late . . . *shush!* How did she sneak up so quietly? Where did she come from? Where does she go when the sun goes down?

Mr. Math With the personality of a squid, he throws numbers at you like algebra really matters. Rubik's Cube is more fun than sex! Rubik's Cube *is* sex!

The exterminator He goes by the title "vice-principal," but don't be fooled. Hang around the hallway one split second past the bell, and poof! You're history.

Ken and Barbie They teach gym. Tan. Wearing shorts. You've probably already noticed . . .

Sid Sociology He's gay. The parents don't know it, but the students do. He encourages his classes to "keep their minds open," unless it involves biblical Christianity, which he refers to as "a nice little crutch for those who need to justify their insecure existence."

The cafeteria crew They're never asked to cook at home. For obvious reasons . . .

The substitute teacher Will be buried with military honors at Arlington National Cemetery. For obvious reasons . . .

Señor Spanish It's important that he thinks you're learning a foreign language.

Send me some teacher types you've noticed. I've got to get to work on my next book. It's just nice to know you can't get AIDS from Rubik's Cube.

Dear Pat,

Why do some teachers look like they don't enjoy teaching at all?

Get a Life

Dear GAL,

There are several possibilities. Maybe they need more bran in their diets. Or maybe they're on a waiting list to work for the IRS. Or it's possible they're wearing their underwear too tight. Or the obvious: It's just a job to them!

You can respond in several ways:

Ignore them, maybe they'll die soon. Problem: These people *never* die.

Be extra nice to them and smile a lot. Problem: They'll think you're on drugs.

Report them to the principal. Problem: He's never at school.

Complain to other teachers. Problem: They'll give you extra homework.

Tell your parents. Problem: They'll tell you how rough their teachers were!

Why don't you and some of your friends simply ask your teacher why he doesn't seem to be enjoying his work. You have a right to know. If it's done gently and sensitively, you may contribute to this teacher's life. The answer may surprise you.

Dear Pat,

I don't like taking tests in school. Do I have any rights as a student?

Wondering If I'll Graduate

Dear Wondering,

Do you have any rights as a student? What kind of question is that? Are you an American? Have you heard of the Constitution? It guarantees four freedoms, remember? Remind your teacher the next time that test is handed out:

Freedom of speech Do teachers let you talk when you take tests? Of course not! Well, maybe they should read their little government books. You can talk to anyone, anytime—especially during tests. Trust me.

Freedom of press Teachers can't tell you what to write. This is America! You've got the freedom to print any opinion on paper. Have fun! Put down any answer you want. No problem.

Freedom of assembly Get all your friends together and take the test as a group. Thomas Jefferson said it was okay, and he was a good friend of George Washington. Your teacher won't dare challenge them.

Freedom of religion If you choose to pray and hold church the day of your test, you have the right. Go ahead, make God's day!

Remember, you're an American! Make us proud, even though you'll never graduate in your lifetime . . .

Dear Pat,

I go to a Christian school.
Everybody there thinks they're
Christians, but they're not. I'm
so frustrated. I want to reach my
friends, but they don't see any
need spiritually.

Not into Labels

Dear Labels,

First of all, not everybody at your school thinks
they have it together spiritually. This is where you begin. Pray that God will lead you to those students
who are willing to listen. Go to them one by one and
see if they want to start a Bible study for the purpose
of reaching out to others in the school. Find a Christian teacher who really is a Christian teacher. He or
she can provide both a room and encouragement as
your growing group begins to happen.

Remember, you're on a mission that is very familiar to God. The Bible tells story after story of
Christians who were tired of settling for religious labels and did something about it. You're a part of
that history, and you'll be making new history.

Read the first three chapters of Nehemiah. He
rebuilt the wall around Jerusalem. You're going to
rebuild the spiritual faith at your school. This is *your*
Jerusalem. Nehemiah said, "You see the bad situation we are in, that Jerusalem is desolate and its
gates burned by fire. Come let us rebuild the wall
of Jerusalem that we may no longer be a reproach"
(Neh. 2:17).

God is ready. Go find your builders. Pray. Be
patient and expect criticism. But keep building up
the city of God.

Dear Pat,

As a Christian, I believe that schools are really run by secular humanists, atheists, New Agers, and communists. Who do you think runs my school?

On Alert

Dear Alert,

Although those people are the lifeblood of every school system, they don't really run the school. The true movers and shakers are the following, in order of importance.

The janitor Surprise! The reason is very simple. What do you throw into the garbage at school? Financial vouchers, district invoices, extracurricular budget disbursements, and the notes you and your friends pass in class. The janitor is *Numero Uno*. He or she can blackmail the whole school. Address them as "Sir" and "Ma'am."

The yearbook editors Go ahead—make them angry. They have the power to print a nice big picture of you with spinach stuck in your teeth for everyone to see (including your children). They *always* have the last laugh. Buy them dinner.

The drum major That big football game can't start until the stupid band gets off the field. Musicians, especially oboe players, love their power.

Any German shepherd They sniff your locker, and you're on your way to prison. Stock up on doggie biscuits or you're dead meat.

The secular humanists are the least of your problems!

Dear Pat,

My locker partner stores drugs in our locker. What do I do?

Caught in the Middle

Dear Caught,

If there are drugs in your locker, you can do one of two things:

1. Go to a hardware store and have them design a beautiful sign that flashes in bright neon: "Drugs." Your locker will look just like all the other pharmacies in town. That'll encourage your locker partner to clean things out fast.

2. You could give him or her a deadline of say . . . ten seconds . . . to get that crap out of *your* locker because:

   - it's illegal
   - it's killing people
   - it's jeopardizing your reputation
   - it's stupid
   - it's causing you to lie

If your locker partner threatens you, say to him or her: "What you do with your life is something I can't control. But what you do that affects my life is just as much my right as yours. I want you to respect that."

Then go see if you can get a new locker partner. You deserve better.

Dear Pat,

I ran for a school office, and I lost. It still hurts. I even have trouble sleeping because I feel so bad. I just feel like a loser.

Defeated

Dear Friend,

Please sit down and really read what I'm about to write. This is very important!

I want you to look at these two circles:

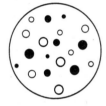 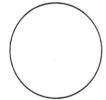

Our performance
(Rom. 7:18)

Christ's performance
(Rom. 5:1–5)

In the circle on the left, you see a lot of smaller circles, both black and white. These little circles represent our performances, both good and bad. The good ones (white, naturally) might include good grades, a new girlfriend or boyfriend, or even winning an election. These are things we think are good performances for us. The bad performances (black) might be drugs, getting kicked out of class, or maybe even losing an election. But if you're a Christian, this circle really doesn't exist. This is how we judge ourselves, good or bad. Jesus Christ has a different standard.

Look at the circle on the right. It's pure, blameless, and totally clean in God's eyes. The reason you're so down is because you're living in the wrong circle. Thank God it's not up to us to please God with our performances!

Dear Pat,

Why are class periods so long?

Bored beyond Belief

Dear BB,

This'll be an easy question to answer because bored people (like you) won't even bother to read this. Anything more than a couple of words will guarantee that you won't discipline yourself to finish reading anything I can write here. You don't care because the answer's too long and therefore a waste of your time and my time.

So that's why I'm filling this page with stuff that doesn't matter. By now you're flipping through the rest of the book and glancing at the television as you listen to your music and wonder what you're going to do tonight.

For now, let's see if we can finish this page with something that'll be totally meaningless, like state capitals: Montgomery, Juneau, Phoenix, Little Rock, Sacramento, Denver, Hartford, Dover, Tallahassee, Atlanta, Honolulu, Boise, Springfield, and Indianapolis. How about something really stupid, like school colors of small colleges: purple and white, red and black, brown and yellow.

It looks like this page is pretty full now. I find it so interesting that, just as there are people who don't read these pages, there are some who read every word. Scary, isn't it?

Dear Pat,

I have a teacher who's an atheist.
As a Christian, do you have any
suggestions on how to open him up
to spiritual things?

Potential Witness

Dear Po,

Tell your teacher that Albert Einstein knew 3 percent of all the knowledge in the universe. Ask your teacher, based on that, how much knowledge he has. If he says, "About as much as Einstein," then draw this for him:

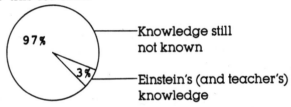

Ask your teacher if it's possible that God could exist in the 97 percent that he hasn't yet experienced. (His answer has to be *yes*.) If someone isn't sure if God exists, then he's not an atheist. Technically, he's an agnostic, or one who isn't sure God exists. Unless he knows 100 percent of all the knowledge in the universe, he can't be sure, right?

Now ask him if he's a *positive* agnostic or a *negative* agnostic. If he wants to know the difference, tell him, "A positive agnostic says, 'If there's a heaven and I can live eternally, I'm interested.' A negative agnostic says, 'Even if there is a God and eternal life, I'm still not interested.'"

Most so-called atheists are really positive agnostics. If your teacher's a negative agnostic, then all you can do is pray and ask God to start opening his heart!

Dear Pat,
Has gym class changed since you
were in high school?

P.E. Man

Dear P.E.,

You wouldn't believe how much it's changed.

We did real exercises None of that fancy aerobic stuff for students of the '60s. We did things that made us sweat. We'd lay out on the hot cement and do sit-ups until our stomachs ached. That was the easy part. The real challenge was to keep moving. Our gym teacher had only one eye. He didn't realize that our exercise area doubled as the test area for the driver training class.

Everyone took showers Today a lot of students don't have to take showers. They don't want to get their hair wet. Not us. We showered every day. That may not sound like a big deal to you, but the whole class had to share one towel . . . made of paper . . . recycled from the cafeteria . . . the day we had fish sticks. The people in the next class thought we'd been chasing Moby Dick.

War games We knew how to compete in our gym classes. People didn't play dodge ball; people *died* playing dodge ball! We'd carry them off, say a prayer, and rush back before the bell rang ending our fun. Guys in my class joined the Marines to get out of gym.

Our coaches were one of a kind Today's gym teachers look fit and trim. Ours looked a lot like the lounge lizards in *Star Wars.* In fact, I think the guys in that bar scene were our coaches.

The "smell" of the locker room This is a little hard to describe on paper. Try to imagine the inside of a camel's mouth after it has eaten hot chili dipped in ether! Then imagine the camel belching. I loved P.E.!

Rainy days   When the weather turned bad, we got to see exciting films like *Why Bee Hives Have Only One Queen* and *The History of Ice.* Or we could volunteer to run to the cafeteria to get the towel for shower duty.

Most memorable moment   My goal in high school was to have hair that looked like Paul Mc-Cartney's. Unfortunately, my hair was curly and kinky and forever destined to keep me separate from Beatlemania. So one day my friend bought me some hair straightener. I rubbed it in real good, and it looked like someone had glued my hair down and covered it with shoe polish. I looked more like a bowling ball than a Beatle.

My first shower in gym made that hair come alive. It smelled like rotten eggs and looked like a blender had gone berserk through it! My hair was frozen in time with jagged edges everywhere, sort of early punk. I was a walking sulphur spring. It took three months to get that stuff out of my hair.

Dating

Why the opposite sex is so weird

Dear Remy,

You may never "forget" this person. Rather than put him completely out of your mind, let's put the relationship completely in focus. What really happened? Were you *really* in love with this person? Was he *really* in love with you? Or . . . were you in love with the *idea* of loving this person? Giving up a romance with a person is harder than giving up the person! Do you tend to remember the good times rather than the bad ones? That's romance. You can have romance with a lot of people. This one just hits you harder right now. You need the following:

Time It has only been a month, yet it feels like a year, right? The first month is always the toughest. It gets easier.

Patience How come nothing is happening? Because you don't need anything to happen right now. The wounds need to heal. You don't need more battles. Just rest.

God's grace Read Rom. 8:26–39 and thank Him for being there through all your pain. Ask Him to show you more verses in the Bible.

Perspective This is not the end of the world. It's not even the end of your life. It's a relationship that you need to learn from. Period. You'll look back and smile someday.

Just remember that all love is not bad . . . just certain romances.

Dear Pat,

There are certain girls at school who would be considered "cheap." Guys really take advantage of them. What could I say to encourage these girls to respect themselves more?

                                                    A Gentleman

---

Dear Sir Walter,

I remember a girl during my junior year. She was in my English class. She was someone all the guys wanted to mess around with on Saturday night and then ignore on Monday morning! She had a great body and a lousy reputation. She liked me, and she trusted me.

One day I went over to her house with a friend, and we played an ancient game called "Spin the Bottle." She had a friend who kept spinning the bottle toward my friend. So when they left the room to kiss, this girl and I would kiss, too. Soon things got out of hand, and I found myself in a bedroom with this girl. She was downing pills like popcorn to calm herself, thinking that *I* wanted serious sex. To be honest, she started taking off her clothes and asked me to go to bed with her. I told her to get dressed, and, as I sat on the edge of the bed, she started crying. She told me that the reason she had moved to our school was because she had made sexual mistakes at her previous school. She wasn't cheap; she was scared. She wasn't "loose"; she was lonely. I never kissed her again. From then on, I tried to be the best friend I could to let her know she was worth far more than a quick grope in bed.

People who don't respect themselves are not limited to the female sex. There are a lot of guys who also cheapen their reputations for the sake of being accepted. "Cheap" women or men deserve God's grace, not more mistakes.

> **Dear Pat,**
>
> I've been spending time with one girl for about two months. I'd like to get more serious. How do I know if God is leading me to intensify the relationship?
>
> The Biblical Dater

Dear BD,

I think it's great that you want to know the principles of scriptural dating. Let's keep it simple and to the point:

This relationship belongs to God The moment you and your girlfriend try to take this "friendship" for yourselves, you're in trouble. God must not only ordain it, He must *own* it. He gave Eve to Adam for the purpose of marriage, and you need to make certain He wants this relationship to get more serious.

Genesis 6 is a prime example of God's men intermarrying with women who did not honor God. The result? A devastating flood that wiped out the earth. God does not share His glory with those who give their hearts to something He chooses not to bless. As you proceed, ask Him for signs that He *is* blessing your growing relationship.

Be constantly filled with the Holy Spirit Ideally, it would be great if neither of you sin in the relationship. However, when you do sin, confess it immediately. Do not let it build up in your life, and do not let it settle into the relationship. The obvious sin is physical sex, but there are a number of other sins that can destroy the relationship just as quickly: jealousy, distrust, selfishness, lying, negativism, insecurity, manipulation, pride, *and* stubbornness.

It is critical that these sins do not get a foothold in your life or between the two of you. They do not glorify God, and they will destroy any potential you have together. When one of them crops up, you can do this:

1. Admit your sin to God (1 John 1:9).
2. Repent (don't keep doing it!).
3. Ask God to heal the spiritual wound.
4. Set up an environment where you don't keep doing it.
5. Ask your partner to help you in that area for your personal holiness and for the sake of your relationship.

Does the relationship continue to glorify God? You'll either draw closer to Him individually and together or you won't. The relationship will never stay in neutral. If it begins to hurt your obedience to Him, it's time to evaluate whether He is blessing it or not. If He's not, the relationship is over.

Is it encouraging you as the spiritual leader? Someday you may be married to this girl. Ephesians 5 says that the husband is to be the spiritual head of the wife as Christ is the head of the Church. Do you see that pattern developing between the two of you now? If it doesn't move in that direction, then you're not biblically moving toward marriage, and you need to get counsel.

Is God confirming the relationship with your parents? Even if your parents aren't Christians, God can still use them to verify or deny the relationship. You'll be spending the rest of your lives with them. No one understands that more than God your Father. My prayers go with both of you.

Dear Pat,

I made a mistake sexually. How forgiven am I?

Scarred

Dear Scarless,

That answer depends on whether you've given your sin to Jesus Christ. If you have, then read John 8:3–11 and pay close attention to the words of our Lord to the woman who sinned sexually: "And straightening up, Jesus said to her, 'Woman, where are they? Did no one condemn you?' And she said, 'No one, Lord.' And Jesus said, 'Neither do I condemn you; go your way; from now on sin no more.'"

From the words of Jesus Christ, we hear the great phrase: "Neither do I condemn you . . ." Are you forgiven? Yes. Completely? Yes, yes! Will you forgive yourself? That's *your* decision.

You made a choice at one time to sin with your body and mind. Now you need to make a choice to claim His total forgiveness for that sin. When He does, do not climb up on His cross and take back that forgiveness.

You're clean and pure once you lay any sin at the cross of Jesus Christ. You have exchanged something impure and unholy for a Spirit of godliness. If Jesus is pure as I write this, and you've claimed Him, then you're as pure as He is—even sexually. Go your way and sin no more in that area, Scarless.

Dear Guy,

Let me tell you a story. One day I was with a very good-looking girl in my apartment. I had strong feelings for her. She really liked me. We began to show our affection for each other. Kissing was not enough. She took off her coat, and we began to physically express ourselves.

Then the phone started ringing. Ring . . . ring . . . ring. I remember thinking, *No!* It continued to ring, and finally I was forced to answer it. It was my roommate who was bored at work. What a time for him to call! Didn't he know that I was expressing my "commitment" to this girl!

By the time I got him off the phone, my friend had her coat back on and was ready to leave. The moment was over. No "physical expression" for us. That phone call saved both of us from making a major mistake. Soon after that we broke up and went our separate ways.

Two years later, I got a wedding invitation from my old roommate. He was marrying a real sweet girl, a girl I used to know, a girl I was with one afternoon when a phone rang. You guessed it!

The next time you think it is right to express yourself physically to someone you "love," just remember that she'll probably belong to someone else down the road.

> Dear Pat,
>
> I really like this girl, but she can't seem to make up her mind. One day she likes me, and the next day she's not sure. What can I do?
>
> The Yo-Yo Lover

Yo Adrian,

The best thing you can do is *nothing.* If she's not sure, then direct pressure isn't going to help. Give her "space" and give her time. Go back to your life and see if she eventually wants to be with you.

In a spiritual sense, Jesus had a similar problem with a man named Peter. It was a constant struggle for Peter to be certain that he loved Jesus Christ. Our Lord gave Peter plenty of time and opportunities to decide if he wanted to follow him or not. Read John 6:66–69, Mark 14:29–31, and Luke 22:61–62.

Now I know you don't plan on impressing anyone by walking on water or raising people from the dead, but you need to live your life whether she decides to be with you or not. She may not feel she's good enough for you. She may be getting pressure from others. She may not be ready for a serious relationship. She may be still holding on to a past boyfriend. There are countless "may be's."

Let her know she's special to you and that you have no intention of using another girl to manipulate her emotions. Then get on with your life and let her come to you when *she's* ready.

If she does, then she'll be sure. If she doesn't, then you'll be sure.

Dear Schizo,

Girls just want to have fun. They want money, credit cards, total freedom, a cute guy, space, a red sports car, smaller hips, their own personal mall, a lifetime supply of every chocolate product ever made, a best friend, a perfect goodnight kiss, rich in-laws, no homework, a new wardrobe, a different nose, and peace in the world.

How's that for starters? What they *need* is another matter.

In any relationship, a girl wants a guy who understands her and knows when and how to communicate with her. She wants to be appreciated, and she likes a guy with a sense of humor who has a sense of purpose for his life. He needs to have high standards and the sensitivity to know when to lead and when to listen. She needs more than just a guy who goes to church; she needs and deserves a man of God. She needs Jesus Christ.

So don't concentrate on worrying about what she *wants*. Be the man in Christ you need to be and give her something to respond to spiritually. If she wants to be with you, then she's worth your spending time with her. If she doesn't respond to you in your walk with Jesus Christ, then quit trying to figure her out. She doesn't know what she wants, and you don't need that kind of confusion in your life.

Dear Pat,

I'm dating a girl who lives in another state. We only see each other a couple of times a year. Will this relationship work?

Missing Her

Dear MH,

It really depends on what state she lives in. Girls who live in South Dakota will always be loyal because they're snowbound most of the year. They're not going anywhere. Neither are girls in Alaska, Maine, or Hawaii. They're stuck, pal! But girls in southern California are a different story—they have a lot of options. They've got the beach, the mountains, and even the sky! They can wander all over the place! To them "loyalty" is waiting fifteen minutes to ride Space Mountain. Now that's commitment! Maybe Delaware would be safe for you.

The real question is: What do you want in a relationship with the opposite sex? If you desire day-to-day communication and the maturing process of growing together, spiritually and emotionally, then a long-distance relationship is *not* for you.

If you like the excitement of separation on a daily basis and the freedom it gives you to not have your partner right there, then this is a perfect set-up for you.

Any relationship will work if God has put His Spirit into it and you are sensitive in responding to each other as Christ loves you. Remember, though, it's tougher to carry on any relationship long distance because that consistent presence is not there. It may get harder than it is now (Prov. 13:12).

Dear Pat,
As a Christian, when it comes to sex, how far should I go?

                Really Curious

Dear *RC*,

    There're a lot of well-meaning Christians who'll tell you that kissing is going too far. There're a lot of well-meaning Christians who say that kissing is okay, but visits to the "petting zoo" are taboo. There're some well-meaning Christians who say virginity should be your goal; anything short of that—although not preferred—is tolerated.

    The Bible? Memorize 1 Cor. 6:18–20 and realize that your body is a temple of the Holy Spirit. If you can conduct your actions with someone of the opposite sex in a way that glorifies Jesus Christ, then you're within the scriptural limits. Once you stop glorifying your Lord by getting too physical, then you've gone too far. If you get six girls pregnant in one month, then my guess is that you've gone way too far.

    Remember, the issue is your personal relationship with Jesus Christ, not what you can get away with.

Dear Pat,

I'm a homosexual. Do you have an
answer for me?

Don't Call Me Bruce

Dear Rocky,

You're not a homosexual. You've *chosen* homosexual behavior. There's a big difference.

The Bible clearly states your real identity as a Christian through the words of the Apostle Paul: "I have been crucified with Christ: and I myself no longer live, but Christ lives in me. And the real life I now have within this body is a result of my trusting in the Son of God, who loved me and gave himself for me" (Gal. 2:20, LB).

You *are* a child of God. You can choose to obey Him and submit your behavior to His Lordship or use it for your own pleasures. Homosexuality is something you do—not someone you are. Just as a heterosexual decides to have sex outside of God's laws, you're making the same kind of decision.

Who are you going to trust? The God who created you, gave His Son for you, and wants to spend eternity with you? Or natural men who want to benefit selfishly from your body and mind and take you further away from the high calling God has for you?

I suggest you get some Christian counseling and make the decision to be faithful to the One who really loves you.

Dear Pat,

Why do guys bluff?

Dear Gettie,

Guys have always acted like they were cool. Early men used to hunt wild beasts with a bow. If they happened to meet a fifteen-foot Grizzly with *no* arrows in their quivers, they would smirk and someone would say, "You're a dead bear!" The bear would run away, and the men would go home and change their underwear.

Today's high-school guy has a new enemy to contend with, namely, image! Fail here, and he feels like a fool for a long, long time. This is ridiculous, of course, because girls prefer a guy who's humble, rather than some self-serving, arrogant jerk.

I had a date for Homecoming, and my girlfriend broke up with me before the big dance. I was devastated, but I didn't want to show her my real feelings. So I coolly said, "Thanks, Gail! This is great news! I had two dates anyway, and the other girl is so much better looking than you are."

She started to cry. I felt like an amoeba. I've never done anything like that again. I realize now that it's okay to be hurt and not feel ashamed about it. It's more important to me to be honest than to look good. It's also easier on the underwear.

Dear Pat,

I'm sixteen and very much in love. I want to get married to my boyfriend who's in the Navy. My parents do not understand. Do you?

Dug In

Dear Dugi,

Do I understand? I understand several things: I understand that you want to marry your boyfriend. I understand that you're sixteen years old. I understand that your parents don't agree with you. I understand that you want someone to understand. So what do we do?

We must decide how important it is to respect your parents for the authority God has given them over you. This is not a marriage issue; this is a family matter. Until your dad walks you down the aisle, you still belong to your current family. God has given them the power to "throw the switch" and turn you loose.

I ignored this truth once. I came within three days of marrying the wrong girl because I didn't listen to her mom, who said, "My daughter isn't right for you." I figured that since her mom wasn't a Christian, I didn't have to listen. I almost made the biggest mistake of my life. The girl I almost married was an outstanding person, but we weren't ready or right for each other. I can see that now.

You've got time on your side. There's no rush. There is no need to take sides. Assume that your parents want the best for you. When they give you their blessing, you'll understand that they've understood you for a long time.

Dear Pat,

My girlfriend and I have been criticized a lot lately about our behavior. People say we can't keep our hands off each other. What's wrong with physically expressing ourselves? We're not sinning!

Frick and Frack

Dear Frick and Frack,

Your actions may not be sinful in themselves, but if other people are having problems with your behavior, then you're sinning by continuing to upset them. Paul said, "But examine everything *carefully;* hold fast to that which is good; abstain from every form of evil" (1 Thess. 5:21-22).

When most people see you and your girlfriend touching a lot, they're *not* thinking:

"Gee, look at the sensitive way they worship God!"

"I am so *impressed* with their walk with the Lord!"

"Now that's how two Christians in love should act!"

"I'm sure they never have a problem with sexual desires!"

It's probable that most Christians watching you would be thinking the opposite of these statements. Whether you like it or not, you're judged by your outward behavior.

I trust you. If you tell me that you and your girlfriend aren't engaged in sexual sin, I believe you. But I encourage you to strengthen your testimony by making the "label" (the outward appearance) as pure as what's inside. God should get the glory by what we do in secret and by what we do in public.

Dear Pat,

I don't trust guys at all! My father let me down, my boyfriend was a jerk, and I'm sick of it! I can't even believe I'm writing to you!

Fed Up!!!

Dear Fedricka,

I take it by your tone that you're a tad frustrated with men. Let's try to put your feelings into perspective before you rent a tank and start mowing down Boy Scout camps.

If you find a cockroach in a box of Frosted Flakes, do you boycott all cereal, all Frosted Flakes, or just that box of Frosted Flakes? If a teacher puts you down unfairly in class, should you end your life, quit school, or transfer to another class where the teacher is more understanding and patient? If a dad disappoints you, your boyfriend abuses you, and you start looking for every guy to be a jerk, is the solution to quit on all men?

Is it fair to you and the opposite sex to say, "I deserve better than this treatment. There are guys out there who do care. I'm going to be patient with them and myself, because living a life of hurt and bitterness is not something I choose to do! I have just had some bad experiences with insecure men who hurt me!"

Smile. Their behavior isn't worth a lifetime of pain for you.

Dear Pat,

My friends don't like my boyfriend. What should I say to them?

                                   Wishing They Understood

Dear Wishing,

What's the deal? Are your friends going out with him, too? How exactly does that work on dates? Which girl does he put his arm around? You or one of them? It must be tough on him.

Your friends are important, and they mean a lot to you. I understand that. But as much as you care about their feelings, it's more important that the Bible approves of him.

If your girlfriends don't like him because he doesn't honor Jesus Christ, then listen to them. They're telling you the truth about God's standards for your life.

But if their reasons are more like, "He's so . . . tacky!" or "He doesn't do anything for me" or "What do you see in him that I don't?" then that is personal taste. It's your preference against theirs.

As a woman of God, you make choices based on the Word of God. As a girlfriend, you decide a man's value by his trust in Jesus Christ. As a friend, you separate sometimes that which God calls you to do and what your friends want you to be.

Just make sure you're living Col. 3:17 (NASB), and that includes more than just your dating life. God will take care of your friends.

Dear Pat,

How do I handle lust?

Looking for Warmth

Dear Looking,

You handle lust the same way you handle fire. You don't! You get away from it very quickly. The longer you touch it, the deeper it burns.

When I was twelve years old, I was an altar boy. I was a very good altar boy—until one day when I was helping with communion. That was the day I leaned on the offering candles. Have you ever caught on fire? I was one moving marshmallow! Instead of stopping and getting help, I ran . . . alone . . . to go somewhere and burn up! Somebody jumped over the communion rail and put out the fire before I was scarred for life.

Lust is a lot like that experience. It approaches us like a friend who wants to bring some warmth and escape from our daily pressures. Before we know it, we're engulfed in its fire and feeling ashamed and alone, not knowing how to put it out of our life.

God created you to be pure and innocent. He did not intend for you to be scarred for life. Don't try to fight this alone. Share your desires with a mature Christian who can help put out the fire. Read 1 Thess. 4:3–4 together and work out a plan that can give you some realistic hope of fighting this enemy.

Dear Pat,

What are the qualities of the ideal girlfriend?

Confused Girl

Dear Connie,

Here are some observations on what I think guys are looking for in a relationship with you:

Strong Christian I used to be a youth pastor, and I noticed that all the party guys would come to church just to date the Christian girls. "Leave them alone," I said. "Why are you hanging around them?" Their answer was classic: "Because they have a quality about them that other girls don't have!" When you really love God, it shows.

Honesty Guys will break up with girls over just one lie. They want this quality very badly in someone they date. Especially when they give their heart to that girl. Always tell the truth.

Fun Most guys are work oriented, and we can get into a rut pretty easily. If a girl has a sparkle in her eye and likes to have a good time, that's refreshing to us guys.

Unconditional love Guys are trained to never show weakness. We want to be able to relax and not have to perform for the girl at our side. Let us know that it's okay to make mistakes and still be a man.

Loyalty It's true that guys are more accustomed to bonding with their friends than girls are to theirs. We look for a similar kind of bond with our partner of the opposite sex. That's why we need to know you're there through thick and thin.

High sexual standards We prefer virgins or girls who have confessed that area of their lives to Jesus Christ and have reprogrammed their hearts and bodies as though it never happened. We want to marry someone pure. We may test you physically, but we are hoping you'll say no. That will make our love, respect, and appreciation for you even greater.

Natural personality Two words are very important for you girls: Be yourself! A guy doesn't want you to be someone else. He likes you for your personality. If you can relax with it, he can relax. It's very important for a guy to relax around his girlfriend. That's the kind of girl he'll marry.

Challenge A guy likes to think there's always a little more that he hasn't achieved. That's true in a relationship. Don't smother him all at once; let him see your many sides gradually. After almost ten years of marriage, it's not only what I know about my wife that impresses me, it's what I find new and challenging that intrigues me. I'll never fully know her, and that's good.

Expressive appreciation Guys like to feel special. Let him know how unique he is to you. Let him know his good qualities. We love to see that admiration in your eyes.

Dear Pat,

What are the qualities of the ideal boyfriend?

Frustrated Guy

Dear Frus,

I think these are some of the most-desired qualities most girls want in a guy.

Strong Christian This quality is appealing to a lot of girls who don't know Christ as well as to those who do. Why is this important? There's a good chance that a man of God will be honest and have higher standards and a sensitive conscience. That, my friend, is very appealing to a lot of girls.

Communication Learn to express yourself and develop your relationship skills. Your girlfriend grew up with Barbie. She learned to articulate a long time ago. You have some catching up to do!

Sense of humor Girls love to laugh. It's non-judgmental, fun, and shows a certain amount of intelligence.

Appreciation Treat her like she's special. Let her know that she's the most important lady in your life. This is not weakness; this is critical to building her personhood.

Self-Control How do you handle pressure? Do you fall apart or does it make you stronger? A sense of confidence, reflected in your being calm and stable, gives her a feeling of security. She needs to know that you don't panic.

Compassion An ability to sense the needs in others is something every girl wants in her man.

There are so many selfish guys out there. Don't be one of them.

Take some chances Women like unpredictability. They like a guy who has some risk in his blood. As long as that risk is exciting and not threatening to her security, you can add some valuable spice to your relationship.

Set goals and follow them A lot of guys have trouble here. They either have no goals ("Hey, let's go to the beach for the 144th day in a row, man!") or they set several goals and never have the guts to follow through with them. Girls can spot a phony pretty quickly. They want a guy who is going somewhere.

Personal humility Being able to say "I was wrong" is difficult for a lot of men. Our pride is shaken when we have to admit we're less than perfect. I want you to go ahead, take that courageous step, and tell her when you've blown it. There *are* some things our dads never taught us.

Love Yes, girls want to be loved and to love others. If you're doing the above things, you will understand this last one a lot better than anything Hollywood teaches.

Dear Pat,

My boyfriend is so quiet and shy. He hardly ever talks. How do I get him to open up?

Living in Silence

Dear LIS,

First, make sure he's not dead. That is very important. If he is breathing, you can work on some ways to get him to respond to conversation: sign language, multiple-choice questions, a hearing aid (maybe he's been talking *softly* all this time!), or a translator (he could be a foreigner). Then, again, you could tell him the truth: A relationship grows on the trust two people share together. If one person isn't sharing, then it's hard for the relationship to develop. Tell him when he opens up that it means a lot to you.

Growing up, he may have felt uncomfortable talking about himself. He might hate the thought of rejection. He may think that what he says will be stupid. Communicate to him that you love him unconditionally as a person, and that he has the freedom to be himself even when it comes to saying what he feels. Read Rom. 8:31–32 together, share some prayer, and thank God that He allows you to be yourselves and that He loves you with your weaknesses.

Dear Pat,

My boyfriend says I have to do "it" with him, or else he's leaving me. What should I tell him?

Barely Holding On

Dear BHO,

Tell your boyfriend to be more specific about what "it" means. Is he talking about taking you, a special creation of God, and doing things to you for his own *personal* satisfaction that are going to affect your mind and memory for the rest of your life?

Or . . . does he mean that a woman's place on this earth is to fulfill the high calling of making sure her boyfriend is always happy by offering her body as a willing sacrifice whether she likes it or not.

Or . . . maybe he means that other girls have been stupid enough to fall for his moronic suggestions, which has deluded him into thinking that he has the IQ of something higher than a cantaloupe.

Or . . . it's possible that the real meaning of life is to meet an incredibly self-centered jerk who takes the God-ordained act of love for two people in a marriage relationship, coats it with guilt and fear, and uses it as a weapon to destroy those he says he loves.

Ask him what he really means. Then tell him that you're saving yourself for God's man. That's what you deserve for the rest of your life. God created you to have the absolute best. There's someone out there who loves Jesus Christ and you a lot more than you are experiencing now.

Dear Pat,

My boyfriend isn't a Christian. I love the Lord, and I feel like He wants me to continue dating Steve. My parents and my youth pastor disagree with me. What do you say?

Determined

Dear Dete,

Emotions are a funny thing. They can convince us of things that may not be true. Your feelings about Steve may be right; you may really love this guy. But your feelings may be wrong, too. This may not be love at all. That is why we have to rely on something more solid than our feelings—the facts.

The Bible is the Word of God. It is true, and it is to be trusted above our feelings.

The Bible says that if you're a Christian, then you belong to Jesus Christ. He owns your heart, your mind, and your body. You don't belong to anyone else.

Your boyfriend, no matter how caring, moral, sexy, or committed to you, doesn't know Jesus Christ personally.

The two of you serve different Gods. Eventually that will become critical to the potential of your relationship with Steve. As long as you serve different Gods, you will take different courses from each other.

You're not stupid. You may be stubborn. You may be independent. You may be loyal. But you're not stupid.

The truth of God's life in you will eventually win out over your emotions. Deep down you already know that. I trust Him, and I trust you. Read Rom. 12:1–2.

Amusements

If I'm having so much fun, why do I have tire tracks on my t-shirt?

Dear Guys,

Although it would be easy to pick the "classics,"
like *Teenage Mutant Ninja Turtles* or *Surf Nazis*, I'm
going to highlight three films that teenagers loved.
Even though they had their good points production-
wise, there were some unbelievable inconsistencies
that could only be called dumb.

Halloween (1978) This classic horror movie was
written by someone with two brains—one demented
and the other dating it! All the way through the
movie, the slasher is quick, cunning, and all powerful. In less than an hour he easily destroys half of the
high-school trick-or-treaters. But when he meets Jamie
Leigh Curtis he turns into a bubblehead!

She stands screaming at a locked front door for
several minutes while he cruises toward her at 1 1/2
miles per hour. This is designed to get us scared.
Naturally, the door opens—just in time—and she
grabs a knitting needle and drills him. (Why he
doesn't get out of the way is a major mystery
to me.) Then she runs upstairs, sees him again, and
hides in a closet! (That's like hiding on the roof from
a tornado!) Finally, she says to the kids hiding in the
bedroom, "Run away and get the cops . . . I'll wait
here in the house!" I decided then that she and the
writers all deserved to die.

Top Gun (1986) Tom Cruise is so good looking
playing volleyball that he puts the Dolby sound and

the spectacular flight scenes on the back burner for most of the junior-high girls in the audience. But on closer examination, the "love story" between Cruise and Kelly McGillis has the depth of a make-up kit. I've paraphrased their verbal foreplay to give you a clear idea of the intelligence of this movie:

TC: Oooh! You teach at the Pentagon. Whoa!

KM: Better than flying your jets upside down, Flyboy!

TC: You think you're hot snot, but you're really cold boogers!

KM: I know you are, but what am I?!

TC: You wanna sleep together?

KM: I can't resist you . . . you hunk!

TC: Baby, baby! Let's lose that lovin' feeling!

KM: Why not? We've already lost any fans with an IQ over 56.

Then, of course, they sleep together amid beautiful photography, sensual music, and sweat. You'd be surprised how many Christians *wanted* these two together.

Dirty Dancin' (1987)   The plot can be best explained by an eight year old from my church: "Girl sleeps with her boyfriend, and it makes her a better dancer! End of movie." I don't think I could describe it better. It's just scary that an eight year old watched this movie enough times to analyze it so well.

Dear Pat,

Any suggestions on how I can get the family car for Friday night?

A. J. Desperate

Dear A.J.,

Yes, there are several things you can do:

Save Newspaper Clippings Any article that shows a teenager in trouble makes *you* look good. On Friday afternoon, drop about sixty of these clippings in your dad's lap and say, "Thanks to parents like you, I turned out all right! You're a great dad! By the way . . . is the car available for a couple of hours?" Works every time, especially if you can find an article about a car blowing up in the garage.

The Power of the Pump Every year when you're asked at your birthday or Christmas, "What do you want, honey?" you reply, "My *own* gasoline credit card!" Once you have this, you have power. Your parents have no reason to deny you the car ever again! Fill it up before you come home. They'll be so excited at a *full* tank, they'll forget that it's *their* money!

The Great Negotiator There are a lot of crummy errands your mom hates to run. Make her an offer she can't refuse: "Mom, I'll drop off the fabric samples to that woman you don't like, if I can have the car Friday night." Your mother will hug and kiss you and *shove* the car keys into your hand!

The Marriage Guilt Game "Dad, you've been working pretty hard. When's the last time you and mom spent the evening alone at home? How about if all us kids get out of here and let you guys just relax?" This works out especially well for your brothers and sisters who get to spend the night away from home. Maybe you could even get the car all night! It depends on how much guilt you can lay on them.

Time Those Tune-ups Every car needs to be serviced. Why don't you make the appointment on Friday? You know how service stations are *always* late. So you pick up the car at closing time and tell your folks to relax on a Friday afternoon. You'll have it home sometime after dinner or so . . .

The Creative Taxi Cabber Every time your brother or sister has a Friday night activity, they'll need a ride. You report for duty. After you drop them off, you've got the car for a couple of free hours! When you bring them home, send them in with the message, "A.J. had to drop off a friend; he'll be home soon." Your parents will be so glad that they got a Friday night off from chauffeuring that it won't be a big deal what time you get back home.

Please Read! A Few Rules.

1. **Never lie.** If you take the car for a short while, always call from somewhere and ask to lengthen your stay. Possession is nine-tenths of the law here. Once you have the car, your parents will usually give you some leeway. Just don't lie to them.
2. **Don't argue or whine.** Always be friendly and cheerful. They would rather give the car to a happy person.
3. **Be pleased with whatever they give you.** They don't *have* to give you the car at all. Enjoy their grace.

Dear Pat,

Has anything exciting ever happened to you at Disneyland?

Mickey

Dear Mickey,

Several weird things have happened to me. For example, on the Pirates of the Caribbean ride, I got off the boat inside the caves and started walking around. A security guard threatened to expel me from the park. What a grouch!

When I was single, I was always looking for good-looking girls. Once on the StoryBook Land ride I spotted a beautiful blonde tour guide. I waited in line for an hour and timed it perfectly as her boat came up. I jumped in just as her boss said "Kathy, why don't you take a lunch break?" I almost died. I had to go through that *stupid* ride again. I have never forgiven Monstro the Whale for that one.

I once talked the helium balloon man into letting me hold fifty of his balloons for a picture. I *thought* I had a grip on those suckers . . . but the picture turned out great!

Then there was the classic night when my best friend and I had an argument, and he left me at the park without a ride home! With only $3 in my pocket, I met three girls on the Tomorrow Land Rockets. We went on a bunch of rides. They drove me to his house later, and I told him, "Look what you missed!" I wound up dating one of the girls for a year.

Dear Pat,

How crazy were you in high school?

Pretty Wild Myself

Dear Wild Person,

I was pretty crazy. My senior Last Will and Testament predicted my future by saying that "Pat Hurley will someday have his own sanitarium!" Pretty encouraging, huh?

After I graduated from high school, I managed to earn a "D" average over five semesters in *junior* college! When I was nineteen, my best friend and I drove to Los Angeles with $13 between us and stayed two months. I dated eight different girls, almost got blown away by a robber in a gas station, got thrown in jail for cussing out a policeman, and threatened to kill a guy in my apartment complex for asking me to sleep with him. I also totaled my car and hitchhiked to work (forty miles) every day on the Los Angeles freeways.

Why did I act so stupidly? Probably because I didn't care about my life that much. If I lived, I lived; if I died, I died.

Jesus Christ has taught me how precious life is when you live it with Him:

> If you have really heard His voice and learned from him the truths concerning himself, then throw off your old evil nature—the old you that was a partner in your evil ways—rotten through and through, full of lust and shame. . . . Yes, you must be a new and different person, holy and good. Clothe yourself with this new nature (Eph. 4:21–22, 24 LB).

I'm so thankful the crazy days are over, Wild Person. So thankful . . .

Dear Pat,

I get depressed very easily. I find that I use my activities to cover up my real feelings of insecurity. Is there anything I should do about this?

Down and Hiding

Dear DAH,

There are some things you should do. First, don't live a lie. Putting pressure on top of pressure can hurt you for life. Admit your depression and don't take on activities that you really don't need to do.

Second, if your depression gets deeper and harder to cope with, go see a Christian counselor who will help you identify the real hurt down inside. Don't just "pray about it"; find the root of where the pain begins.

Third, realize that some depression is from God. He brings it to us to slow us down, give us some rest, and remind us of our dependency on Him. David wrote about this: "I waited patiently for God to help me; then he listened and heard my cry. He lifted me out of the pit of despair . . . and set my feet on a hard, firm path and steadied me as I walked along" (Ps. 40:1-2, LB).

You're not the first person to get depressed, and you won't be the last. But God does hear you, and He wants to heal you completely. Start by getting some help.

Dear Pat,

What do you do when you're bored?

Adventurous

Dear Advent,

There are two types of boredom: one that takes our lives out of gear with no excitement in sight, and one that occurs once in a while during the day or night. There are solutions for both.

In 1979, I felt my life going nowhere. I wasn't really happy doing anything. I began to pray for a major career change. I was *lifetime bored!*

One Sunday morning, I flipped on the television and saw a program called "Kids Are People, Too!" I said to myself, "Self, you could do stand-up comedy on that show!" The real question was whether God wanted me to proceed specifically in that direction. I went through my biblical checklist for God's Will:

1. Was I seeking God's best? Yes.
2. Was there sin in my attitude? No.
3. Was I delighting myself in the Lord? Yes.
4. Did this match up with my desires and gifts that God had given me? Yes.
5. Was I in a position to go for it? Yes!

So I called ABC-TV the next day, and they asked for a video demo. My life took a major career change that day as I entered the world of secular television. Since then I have worked for three television stations, done several commercials, and received two Emmys. Am I bored careerwise? No. Why? Because I took some chances and realized that God wants me to be *all* that He created me to be (Jer. 33:3).

Do I get bored at times during the day? Yes. It is a fact of life that there will be times when nothing is happening. What do I do? Several things:

1. Call a friend.
2. Think of a project I've always wanted to do.
3. Take a nap.
4. Grab my remote control and start flipping.
5. Read my Bible or just talk to God.
6. Jog.
7. Eat something chocolate.
8. Read a chapter of a book.
9. Write a letter.
10. Play electronic games.

It's not important *what* you do; it is significant to note that the moment you get involved in something, you quickly lose that bored feeling and start to feel better about yourself.

God gives us moments of boredom to take us out of gear, to give us a chance to rest up for the next activity in which He has called us to be involved. Enjoy your moments of peace and quiet. They give you the energy for the pressures of life.

I'm more concerned about an overall goal for my life. If I'm bored there, then I'll have problems. The gaps in my day don't bother me as much as my struggle to feel significant with my life.

Dear Pat,

Is drinking wrong? Some Christians believe it is, and some believe it isn't. What's the deal?

"Spuds"

Dear "Spuds,"

Drinking is wrong if:

You're Underage Jesus said, "Obey your government" (see Matt. 22:21), and if you're not of drinking age or you're drinking at home without the permission of your parents, then you're sinning.

You Drink Too Much The Bible clearly states, "Do not get drunk with wine, . . . but be filled with the Spirit" (Eph. 5:18). Even if you're an adult, you sin by drinking too much.

You Cause Your Brother to Stumble (see Rom. 14:15–21, LB) I remember the time I ordered a drink in a restaurant after spiritually ministering to a young Christian. He threw all my "advice" back at me when he said, "Some man of God you are! You're a hypocrite!" I wasn't sensitive to the fact that *he* believed drinking alcohol was wrong for a Christian. I never forgot that experience.

You Hurt Your Testimony to Unbelievers (see Matt. 5:16, LB) Non-Christians watch us. They check us out to see if we are consistent in our witness for Jesus Christ. There are many who would see us drinking and think less of our Lord as a result.

Is it ever possible for a Christian to drink? I know a good many who do. I respect them and their walk with the Lord. They do not fit in the above categories, and they do not let it come between them and their relationship with God.

Dear Crete,

It's admirable that you are willing to sacrifice
your Friday and Saturday nights for the sake of the
gospel. Now let's get *really* honest for a moment.
Why do people go to parties? List the real reasons:

To escape the pressures of the week
To get wasted
To pick someone up
To have a really good time with friends
To hear the Word of God from you

The last one doesn't quite fit, does it? Nice try.
There are plenty of other opportunities for you
to share your faith with people in situations where
they would welcome a caring approach.

If you happen to be at a party, I would encourage you to evaluate your motives for being there.
Size up the situation, and then maybe leave with
someone who "feels like talking." Scripture is more
comfortable with that: "We try to live in such a way
that no one will ever be offended or kept back
from finding the Lord by the way we act, so that
no one can find fault with us and blame it on the
Lord" (2 Cor. 6:3, LB).

Unbelievers don't expect strong Christians to
hang around parties. As men and women of God,
we should have **higher** expectations for ourselves.

Dear Pat,

My friends and I like to cruise around on the weekends looking for good-looking women. Got any "expert" advice?

Hot to Trot

Dear Trotter,

Here are some sure-fire tips to pick up women[*]:

Get a Cruise Mobile! Women always notice the kind of car you drive, so get something really sharp . . . like your parents' station wagon. Girls love something with a luggage rack. Really.

Your Fellow Cruiser It's important that your buddy be uglier than you. This will guarantee the best-looking girl for yourself. However, if there are a bunch of you, and you're the only good-looking one, you might as well stay home. No girl wants to go out with a guy who's president of the Elephant Man Club.

Clever Phrases Girls love it when you yell out the window of the car. Especially when you say things like, "Hey, Babe! That body should be illegal!" or "Wooo, lookin' good! Yeah!!!" There is no way girls can resist those lines. Guys who talk like that are incredibly sexy . . . in their own minds.

Cruise with Confidence Whenever other guys pass your car, *always* give them a sly wink! That will let them know two things: that you have all kinds of girls chasing you and that you're lying! But that's okay, because it's when you realize that you don't have to be something you're not that girls really do want to get to know you.

[*]According to construction workers who've had at least five beers and no sleep for three days.

Dear Pat,

Why do guys always brag about getting drunk?

Grossed Out

Dear Grossica,

They do brag, don't they? Like the ancient warriors who went out to do battle and came back telling of their incredible conquests, these modern-day Huns are just as proud of their excursions into Stupid Land.

The drunkest I ever got was not something I ever bragged about. I combined a six-pack of beer with a pint of bourbon in about 10½ minutes. All my friends were chanting Go! Go! Go! So I went, went, went! After driving around for a while, we went to a dance.

By this time my stomach was churning, my head was weightless, and I felt like I was in someone else's body. Then I asked a girl to dance. I'll never forget the smile on her face. First, she began to laugh softly. Then she started giggling. At this point I began to get concerned. What was so funny?

I looked down at myself and realized I had been throwing up without even knowing it. By the time I left her, she was laughing hysterically. I staggered into the bathroom and announced to everybody, "Hi, guys!" They took one look at me and scattered like ants who had just seen their first human foot! I went out to a friend's car and laid down to rest for a couple of hours. My friend sold his car soon after that . . .

Was I proud of what I did? Nope. Was it something I would do again? No chance. Why didn't I brag about it? Because I want my life and my name to mean something more than a night of selfishness.

Dear Pat,

I'd rather stay home and read instead of going out on dates with guys. Is there something wrong with me? My friends think I'm crazy.

Not Typical

Dear Typpy,

I don't think there's anything wrong with you at all! Life is full of choices, and at this point you have *chosen* to spend it intellectually instead of socially. Here are a few things to think about during this time.

The kind of books you're reading say something about you. For example, if you're not excited about dating, but you're reading a lot of romance novels, that suggests that you may be waiting for your "handsome prince" to come along. If you're reading biographies, then you're looking for personal ideas on how to make your life count. If you're reading mysteries, perhaps you're looking for excitement in your life. Check it out. What you read says a lot about you.

Make certain your books aren't a substitute for real-life issues. How we spend our leisure time is our business. But we have a God-given need to be with people (Gen. 2:18), and there is a fine line between our personal enjoyment of things and isolating ourselves from the world. Just make certain you understand that difference. Don't hide behind your books.

When you spend time with a guy, you'll have something significant to talk about! I'm glad you're a reader. You're building depth where a lot of people have a canyon! I'm proud of you. It's going to be a fortunate young man who spends time with you!

Dear Pat,

**Are weekend parties as great as
everyone says they are? I'm a
Christian, and I don't go.**

Missing Out

Dear MO,

You're not missing anything. Don't consider the excitement level of a party animal; consider the source! Is this the kind of person you'd trust with your money or your life?

I used to go to parties in high school and college. In some cases, I *was* the party. Before I became a Christian, I used to party pretty well . . . me and the cast of characters who still typify most parties today. They include:

The guy sick in the bathroom He would lie there in agony just moaning his pain away! "Oh-h-h-h . . . ," he would cry. We'd yell encouraging things to him like, "Hey dude, if you get sick . . . just roll inland!" Then we'd point to the toilet that stood as a reminder that certain things were never meant to be inside our bodies!

The couple who's always fighting! Isn't there always a guy and his girlfriend who break up at least once a week, usually at parties? He would sit on the front porch, and all of us would say, "Man, you're free! All the women in this place want you! They'd die for you!" All lies, of course, but he was so drunk that he bought it!

His girlfriend would sit in the bedroom surrounded by all her friends who said in their nasal voices, "You don't need him! You don't, you really don't!" Of course, in their minds they were all saying, "*I* need him! He's such a fox. She's *so* stupid!"

The redneck wrecking crew There're always three guys sitting on the kitchen counter eating all the food in someone else's house. "Great stuff, mmm!" they mumble while scarfing down huge loads of turkey, ham, and cinnamon rolls and stuffing their faces so fast they could seriously injure themselves for life! I was amazed they could breathe!

The freaked-out host Every time a headlight appeared on the road, the guy hosting the party went into a frenzy! "It's my parents! It's . . . the cops! . . . It's a gang!" He was sure something terrible was about to happen! We always told him to relax. This was easy for us to say; the place looked like it'd been nuked by a brewery, and we were leaving to go level someone else's place. Of course, we thought he was uptight; it wasn't our homeowner's insurance.

The girl with the laugh Every party has a girl whose laugh permeates the whole house. It shatters your eardrums, but it tells you the party is in full blast. Once she leaves, the party's over.

I guarantee that things like this still go on. Are you missing much? Maybe a chance to get high, an opportunity to make a drunken fool out of yourself, and an experience that could land you in jail. Certain experiences are not worth trying. There are no winners here—mostly people pretending they aren't losers.

Am I saying don't ever go to parties? No. I'm saying that if you go, keep your mission in mind. Don't be impressed or taken in by the good times! Remember that Jesus Christ goes wherever you go.

Dear Pat,

Should I say something to a drunk friend who's getting ready to drive home?

Reluctant to Offend

Dear Offie,

If someone is drunk and about to drive away, you don't have to say much—just take the car keys away from them!

If you don't know them, go to one of their friends and announce, "Your friend is drunk and about to drive home. You have two choices: Take the keys and have someone sober drive him or watch me call the police. Something probably won't happen, but it might, and it's not worth the chance."

Ephesians is clear on our stance as Christians: "So be careful how you act; these are difficult days. Don't be fools; be wise: make the most of every opportunity you have for doing good. Don't act thoughtlessly, but try to find out and do whatever the Lord wants you to. Don't drink too much wine, for many evils lie along that path; be filled instead with the Holy Spirit, and controlled by him" (Eph. 5:15–18, LB).

Friends are important. We should love them. We should want to be a testimony to them that Jesus Christ loves them. Sometimes that means doing something tough. It will not always be easy or popular, but it may change their lives. It might at least save them.

Dear Pat,

What's so great about the prom?

Dateless So Far

Dear Dateless,

There are a lot of great things about your prom that you'll remember forever, but overindulgence is not one. When you let things get out of control, those "great" memories get slanted into one big nightmare.

You get to spend a lot of money! When you add up flowers, tux or gown, dinner, dance, breakfast, limo, incidentals, etc., you could easily blow $300 to $500! Or you could get your parents to pay by suggesting: "Gee, a Prom only comes along once in a lifetime . . . Hint, hint."

You get to be nervous! There's nothing that puts sweat on anyone's palms quicker than a prom! Everything *must* be perfect! Since you're not, grab the baby powder! That first time you meet your date's parents is one wet thrill!

You get your picture taken at the dance! This is especially neat when you and your date break up three days later, and the pictures arrive with a bill for $100! Yes, sir!

You get to compare yourself with everyone else! You think Miss America pageants are tough? Check out women at a prom! They're noticing dresses, corsages, jewelry, kind of limo, postdance choices, and, of course, the young men who accompany them! This stuff is *more* important than the prom!

You get to dance in real comfortable clothes! Have you ever seen penguins on stilts? Then you've been to a prom!

You get memories for life! I fell asleep on my date at the prom. I'll never forget that. I spent $94 in one hour. I'll never forget that. My feet hurt for a week. I'll never forget that. But what the heck: proms only come once in a lifetime! For most people that's *plenty!*

Dear Pat,

Define "pornography," please.

All Eyes

Dear Al,

You're asking me to define something that the Supreme Court of the United States isn't able to do? Sure, no problem:

This could be pornography. Am I kidding? Slightly.

If what we see can be combined with habits from our old nature, past sexual experiences, and dressed up seductively by the world, then we can take a clothing catalog and turn it into *Penthouse* magazine! The Bible says, "For all that is in the world, the lust of the flesh and the lust of the eyes and the boastful pride of life, is not from the Father, but is from the world" (1 John 2:16). Of course, if we're already reading *Penthouse*, we don't need the help of the other forces, do we? Yes, that's pornography.

The Supreme Court basically said, "Pornography is in the eyes of the beholder." They say it is an individual perception. The Word of God says that anything that debases or dehumanizes God's creation is sin. Men or women exposing themselves outside of marriage is not what God intended for pleasure. Sin, by any other name, is still sin!

Instead of worrying about the concept of pornography, we would be better off concentrating on purity. That is always uplifting to any man or woman.

Dear Pat,

Why do girls go to the mall?

A Girl Watcher

Dear Gwatch,

Girls go to malls for several reasons:

To get out of the house! Girls want to get away from boring family life and hang out in air-conditioned rooms, eat junk food, try on clothes, and listen to music constantly . . . stuff they could never do at home!

To check out guys! There are young men everywhere! They work at the mall, they shop at the mall, they hang out at the mall, and some of them even rob the mall! Yes, sir, a guy for every girl!

To visit the food fair! Every mall has a circle of fast-food places that is fun to visit. It's a treat to sample as many different foods as possible! It's even more of a treat when you bring Alka-Seltzer and Kaopectate! No question about it.

To spend money! The first two words little girls used to say were "mama" and "dada." Times have changed. The two most important words now are "Charge it!" Move over parents, here comes the Gimmee Generation! Flash that plastic . . .

To get exercise! Girls can walk ten miles on a given Saturday. A mall exercise video would put Jane Fonda to shame. Of course, girls need to do all that walking . . . after the food fair.

Dear Pat,

What do you think about dancing?

Footloose and Fancy Free

Dear Footloose,

What do I think about dancing? Well, since I look like a retarded rhino careening down a glass mountain on track shoes, I usually stay off the dance floor! I'd probably kill someone if I really got rolling —or seriously impair somebody for a long, long time!

What do I think of you dancing? I have a few thoughts:

If your dancing is not glorifying to God, it's sin. If by dancing fast you're causing others to focus on your body, and by dancing slow you're causing yourself to focus on your partner's body, then it's time to sit your body down!

Most dancing is not glorifying to God. The beat of the music, the sometimes-sexual lyrics, the movement of your body, and the fantasy all of these create *can* produce a "warmth" that may encourage you to forget about Jesus Christ and focus on your personal desires.

Be real honest with yourself and with God. I know most high-school students dance. I also know most high-school students don't worship Jesus Christ as a way of life. It comes down to the kind of relationship you have with Christ and the standards you set for yourself.

```
Dear Pat,

Sometimes I think God wants to take
away all my fun. Tell me it isn't
true!

                Looking over My Shoulder
```

Dear Shoulder,

It's just the opposite: sin is trying to take away all your fun, and God is trying to free you from sin.

"Jesus answered them, 'Truly, truly, I say to you, everyone who commits sin is the slave of sin. And the slave (sin) does not remain in the house forever; the son (Jesus) does remain forever. If therefore the Son shall make you free, you shall be free indeed'" (John 8:34–36).

Sin is not fun. It starts out exciting sometimes, but eventually guilt, shame, resentment, bitterness, loneliness, depression, and confusion overwhelm us, and we are trapped by our own selfishness. That's not fun.

The Bible says, "In those days when you were slaves of sin you didn't bother much with goodness. And what was the result? Evidently not good, since you are ashamed now even to think about those things you used to do, for all of them end in eternal doom. . . . But the free gift of God is eternal life through Jesus Christ our Lord" (Rom. 6:20, 23b, LB). You stay away from sin, and you won't believe all the "fun" you'll start having. Freedom from pain *is* fun!

Dear Pat,

Did Jesus have a good time? I mean, I never see Him smiling or enjoying Himself. Did He?

Just Wondering

Dear J.W.,

Yes, Jesus Christ had a good time. We are not able to see the depth of it because the Bible focuses on His mission in life—not His weekend activities!

It is very important to note that Jesus is sinless. His "good times" did not mean that He did anything that brought dishonor to God the Father (2 Cor. 5:21). That is how we go to heaven, by receiving Him into our lives. God sees us as "sinless" because Christ has replaced our sinful nature with His pure and blameless Spirit.

Did He have a good time on earth? You bet! How do I know? There are several reasons:

Direct references John 2:1–10 tells of a wedding feast where Jesus used the celebration as the occasion for His first miracle. In John 1:38–39, Jesus spends the night talking with two new friends who later turn out to be lifelong followers! They had a great time sharing their lives that first evening. I don't think they played "let's see who can stay up the latest!" but they found other things to laugh about. In Luke 24:13–32, Jesus walked on the road to Emmaus with two of the disciples. They thought Jesus was dead, and they related this to their "friend" walking with them. Evidently their conversation was very meaningful to them, because when they reached their destination, they invited Him to stay for dinner. Does that tell you something? After breaking bread, Jesus disappeared, and they said, "Were not our hearts burning within us while He was speaking to us?" Jesus **was** exciting to be with. He still is.

Indirect references How do you feel when someone at church or in your youth group comes to know Jesus Christ? Are you happy? Are you having a good time? Miracles usually make us feel very good. Well, the disciples did a lot of rejoicing because there were plenty of miracles to get excited about! Do you think Peter was depressed the night Jesus brought in so much fish that **both** of Peter's boats were sinking? Did Peter and the other disciples ever share a laugh about Peter's little "stroll" on the lake? The chances are that they smiled a tad over that one! How can we assume that? Because *we* joke about it in our sermons. The disciples were no different than us.

We are made in the image of God (Gen. 1:26–27) Do we have a sense of humor? Yes! Do we like to have a good time? Yes! Yes! Are we capable of having a fun time without sinning? Yes! Yes! Yes! Who else is capable of doing that? God the Father, God the Son, and God the Holy Spirit.

We tend to think of Jesus as a one-dimensional person. Always serious. Super intense. Not very fun. Nothing could be further from the truth. Several times a day, I sense Him smiling at me. I just smile back and say, "It would have been great to have spent three years with you on earth!" Then I realize, I've got eternity with Him! And I smile even more.

Potential

My parents should have left me at
the hospital

Dear Pat,

I'm very conscious of my physical appearance. As I look around, I don't measure up very well. Any advice for this ugly person?

Run over by a Semi

Dear Semintha,

So you would never qualify for the cover of a beauty magazine, huh? Welcome to the crowd. The 100 percent crowd. That's right, I've never met anyone who thought they were attractive in high school. None. Zero. Zip. Double Nada! Why? Because we're all products of Adam's sin in the Garden of Eden. You remember that one, don't you? The one that guaranteed physical imperfection until God calls us home for eternity.

Then to Adam He said, "Because you have listened to the voice of your wife, and have eaten from the tree about which I commanded you, saying, 'You shall not eat from it';
Cursed is the ground because of you;
In toil you shall eat of it
All the days of your life . . .
Till you return to the ground,
Because from it you were taken;
For you are dust,
And to dust you shall return" (Gen. 3:17, 19b).

I wish I were 6'2" with blond hair. I would settle for 6'2" *with* hair. But no number of television commercials or music videos, no amount of physical exercise will make me believe I'm physically attractive. I'm first and foremost a spiritual creation, waiting for God to complete me in glory someday.

```
Dear Pat,

I'm afraid to take chances because
I'm really afraid that I'll lose.
Will knowing God better help me
reach out for the decisions I need
to make?
                        Just a Human
```

Dear Human Being,

Take a look at Rom. 8:32. Maybe this poem will help you:

> Some people say that love
>   is a gamble
> They say don't get involved
>   because you might lose . . .
> That is true
>   Losing *is* an alternative
>   in a love relationship
> There is no guarantee
>   that you will win
>   that love will come to you.
>
> Some people say
>   that God
>   took the greatest chance of all
>   when He sent
>   His only Son
>   to die on the cross
>   in our place
>   for our sins . . .
> Some people say
>   His gamble failed . . .
>   They say . . . He lost.

I say He won
I love Him
That is why . . . I can love you
And let others worry
about losing . . .

Dear Pat,

I've been thinking seriously of suicide.

Fading Fast

Dear Fading,

Every night that I'm home, I go into our den after dinner and watch my little girl read her books and play with her toys. I say to myself, "I hope someday she realizes how much I love her." I know there'll come a day when she may not feel very loved. I want to be there for her when that happens because I do love her so very much. I would be hurt if anything ever happened to her.

You see, Corie Elizabeth is a very special girl. Before she was born, we had to rush her mother to the hospital because Corie almost came into this world too soon. She might not have lived if the doctors hadn't delayed her birth by several weeks.

Whenever I think about that, tears come to my eyes. I'm her father, and I care about her very much. As I write this, Corie's playing with a new doll. She's caring for it as though it's the most important person in the world. Someday she'll have her own child. I hope and pray that she'll love that child as much as I love her.

There's someone in this world who loves you, Fading. There's someone who's waiting to be loved by you someday. You just don't realize it right now. Your life *is* valuable, and your presence on this earth is treasured by someone who loves you and who's waiting to be loved by you. You were somebody's baby once. God gave you life. Don't trade in that life selfishly.

Dear Pat,

How can anyone say I have potential when I'm sixteen, pregnant, and living in a foster home?

It's Over

Dear Overa,

Your life's not over, it's resting. You need some time to think about what to do next and who to trust, but you don't need to give up. Think about that child of yours.

There was once a young woman like you who got pregnant without a husband, and she thought over all the decisions she needed to make. One of her choices was abortion. "If I get rid of the baby, I can start my whole life over," she thought. "It'll be like I was never pregnant."

But this young woman knew that her baby had as much right to life as she did, so she made a decision to have her baby. After the child was born, the father decided to marry her and raise the baby in a family environment. The young mother was overjoyed. Her nightmare was coming to an end. She was especially glad she didn't kill the baby. So am I. That woman was my mother.

To this day my mom has had her share of problems. She refuses to give up because she realizes that everyone has problems and everyone has the potential to trust God with them. You deserve that, and so does your baby.

Dear Pat,

Once in a while I cheat on tests. As a Christian, I know any cheating is wrong, but the pressure to get good grades is incredible. Do you understand?

Fudging

Dear Fudge,

Yes, I understand. Every Christian, including me, has cheated on some test in life. We all want to look good at one time or another. My special time came during a summer semester in college.

I had to take biology a second time in order to qualify for graduation. A couple of guys in my class were also having difficulty with this "science kind of thing." They came up with a plan to sneak into the lab the night before the test and copy all the specimens as they lay upon the tables. It was a perfect way to ace the biggest test of the semester. It was also wrong.

The Lord hates cheating and delights in honesty. Proud men end in shame, but the meek become wise. A good man is guided by his honesty; the evil man is destroyed by his dishonesty.
(Prov. 11:1–3, LB)

I took the test the next morning with all the right answers memorized. I deliberately missed most of the right answers because I knew it was cheating. I got a "D" on the test. If I had been a Christian then, I would have asked for a new test because my character is more important than a false college credential.

Dear Pat,

I'm struggling with drugs. I know
they're wrong, but I keep going
back to them. Can you help?

Trapped

Dear Trapped,

There's a way out if you follow through on a couple of things. Remember, this is your life, so take this advice seriously. If you don't, no one can help you.

Step One: Admit you are helpless Don't lie to yourself here. If you pretend you can solve your problem without help, you have no hope. Sit down and tell God that you're tired of lying.

Step Two: Get away from your drug friends These people aren't your friends, they're more interested in drugs than they are in you. They want to escape from their problems, and they will continue to take drugs to do that. You need to escape from them.

Step Three: Get treatment for your problem This is nothing to be ashamed of. If you're sick, you go to a doctor. You're sick right now, and you need to see a doctor, too. Ask someone you trust to go with you.

Step Four: Don't give up Stick with the treatment and do what your counselor tells you to do until you get control of this problem. Keep fighting for your life. Get rid of the poison. There are still some dreams for you to live for.

Dear Pat,

Why are winning and losing so important?

A Product of America

Dear American,

Winning and losing are the twin gods of a country that boasts "In God We Trust." In politics, sports, business, education, and even churches, we're judged by numbers. Every profession has a scoreboard, and every one of us is evaluated by our totals, sometimes on a daily basis.

Are you a failure if you don't get perfect grades? Of course not. Are you a winner because your after-school job makes you more money than your friend? No. Are you a loser when you get cut from the team? Absolutely not. Are you a success when you land a date for the prom with the love of your life? Only for a time.

We need to get off the scoreboard. Our life is not about success or failure, despite what you've been programmed to believe. Relax. The game's over. It ended before it began for us as Christians:

> But you are a chosen race, a royal priesthood, a holy nation, a people for God's own posses-sion, that you may proclaim the excellencies of Him who has called you out of darkness into His marvelous light (1 Pet. 2:9).

This may not be the funniest or most exciting page in the book, but it's the truest. You belong to an eternal God. Let others worship winning and losing.

Dear Pat,

What are the keys to realizing my potential?

Hungry

Dear Hung,

Here are a few of the things I've always applied to my life:

Make certain your dreams are God's dreams for you What good is any success if it's not built upon the Throne of Grace? If God isn't pleased with it, then you shouldn't want it either.

Persistence Never give up! If God has called you to accomplish something, don't let anything stop you. It's said that Jesus "set His face like a flint to Jerusalem," and He never let up until He fulfilled all of His promises. I want to be like that in the mission God calls me to deliver.

Take some chances Risk usually builds character. It makes you stronger because it guarantees a certain amount of failure. Don't be afraid to try something you've never done before.

Today is always the first day of your life Don't spend time looking back and seeing past mistakes or successes. Live today as though your life has just begun, and you'll be open to God's plan for you that day instead of re-beating yourself with failure.

Pray constantly Don't act so humble; you're never that great. He is. So pray without ceasing.

Dear Pat,

My dad says he'll pay for my college if I go to the one of his choice. I don't like his choice. What shall I do?

No Alumnus of Dad

Dear Alum,

There are two answers here. The first answer is the obvious one: Go to the college of your choice and pay your own way. It's going to be tougher for you, but you're not a child. To give in to his ultimatum could cause resentment for years between the two of you. That's not healthy, is it?

The second answer is related to your dad's ultimatum. Why's he doing this? This isn't his college education, it's yours. Why's he putting a dividing line here? It sounds like a deeper problem than just an argument over colleges.

It would be a good idea for you to sit down with him and talk over the whole thing. I suggest an opening like this: "Dad, I'd like to talk to you about college. I want to understand why we disagree on this. I don't want to argue. I want to listen to your ideas on this. I want to work this out." If the two of you can't work it out, I suggest you sit down with a third party, someone who would be fair to both of you, someone you and your dad trust.

Dear Pat,

How do I figure out God's will?

Stuck in the Clouds

Dear Cloudette,

This is simpler than you think. God wants you to know His plan for your life. He didn't create you to confuse you. Try this method from the Bible.

Go to Him with a pure heart Make certain your life is free from sin. Confess and repent of any sins that separate you from God. You must go to Him "clean."

Be prepared for His answer—not yours God will give you direction. Will you accept it? It's very important that you realize His will is more important than your preferences.

His will is usually logical David says, "Delight yourself in the Lord; and he will give you the desires of your heart" (Ps. 37:4). It's like 1 + 1 = 2. Logical. He gave you certain talents and ideas that work well for your personality and goals. When you're trusting Him with those talents, He'll allow you to enjoy it! It's sin that warps this process and makes us think that God wants us to do the exact opposite of who we are as people.

Verify His leading with a mature Christian This is always a good move. It protects you from misunderstanding God's view of you.

Go for it Once you've put your request in and "sensed" His direction, do it. If you're wrong, God'll let you know pretty quickly. Enjoy His will. Don't be afraid of it.

Dear Pat,

What's the average life span of
people today? I mean how long will
I live?

Breathing Hard

Dear BH,

There's a chart especially geared to high school students that can show you how much time you have left. This is a very special chart. Add or subtract the following figures from 74 (male) or 80 (female).

If you take algebra, **add** 2 years.
If you take geometry, **add** 2 years.
If you take out a freshman, get used to disappointment!

If you belong to a club, **add** 1 year.
If you belong to a gang, **subtract** 10 years.
If you belong to shop class, **subtract** 20 years.

If you go to the bathroom alone, **add** 1 year.
If you go to the bathroom in a herd, **add** 5 years.
If you quit going to the bathroom, **add** bran.

If you date an ugly girl, **add** 2 years.
If you date a good-looking girl, **subtract** 2 years.
If you date a gorgeous girl, don't run for president.

If you go to an all-girls school, **add** 2 years.
If you go to an all-boys school, **subtract** 2 years.
If you substitute teach, **subtract** 25 years.

I hope you enjoyed the chart. I made it up myself. Have a nice life.

Dear Pat,

Would you define "success"?

Confused by the Hype

Dear Hypo,

The American Dream says that success is making a lot of money, living in a big house, going on fancy vacations, and being so happy you could spit!

The American Dream is wrong. If you don't believe me, go ahead and have your heart attack now and get it over with.

As Christians, we're called to let Jesus Christ do the work and enjoy the reward. He wants to take credit for both the successes and the failures in life. My favorite verse in the Bible sums this up: "For it is God who is at work in you, both to will and to work for **His** good pleasure" (Phil. 2:13).

If it is His good pleasure to give you a high-salaried job someday, then so be it. If He wants you to marry and have a big house, then He'll take the glory for it.

You work hard with all the talents He has given you; let Him worry about the results. God is neither a capitalist nor a communist. He's Creator and King. When He says "jump," America and the world say, "How high?"

Is that successful enough for you?

> Dear Pat,
>
> All my life I've been the model
> Christian. But lately I've felt
> that it would be fun to experience
> the "other side." I don't want a
> sermon; I want you to understand
> why I'm doing this. Do you?
>
> > Looking for Fun

Dear Fun,

Let's talk like two adults here. I do understand why you're doing this. All those years of doing good and all those sacrifices you made were choices that you felt were important. Maybe your reasons for doing good weren't perfect, but something made you want to be moral and accepted. You chose not to be a bad person or a sinful one. Now you're thinking about changing that choice.

The question is: To whom do you belong? Are you your own person? Do you live for your parents? Your friends? Since you consider yourself a Christian, I'm going to suggest a thought from your Bible:

> For His Holy Spirit speaks to us deep in our hearts, and tells us that we really are God's children.

> Haven't you yet learned that your body is the home of the Holy Spirit God gave you, and that he lives within you? Your own body does not belong to you. For God has bought you with a great price. So use every part of your body to give glory back to God, because he owns it.
> > (Rom. 8:16; 1 Cor. 6:19–20, LB)

No sermon. Just facts. You're not a child anymore. You're an adult, and you must decide to whom you belong.

Dear Pat,

I'm adopted. Even though I love my "parents," I want to meet my real mom and dad. This is putting a lot of pressure on our family. What should I do?

Incomplete

Dear Inky,

Let's define "parents." Is it a mom and dad who produced you physically without taking any responsibility from there? Is parenthood defined by those who took you as a baby, shaped your values, set your standards, and provided for your physical and emotional needs? That latter definition sounds more like your real parents to me.

Going back to the past and finding the people who brought you into this world is satisfying to some people and hurtful to most. Why? Your lives weren't shared over those years, and you're strangers in almost every sense of the word. There's usually a big letdown when you realize that you have nothing in common. They didn't have a child out of responsibility or mutual commitment; they made a mistake. Instead of aborting you, they gave you life. That's a tribute to their character, not a reason for finding them and also hurting the real parents with whom you now live. Those who gave you birth have chosen to keep their lives separate. You need to respect that and not take it personally. This is their issue, not yours.

Whatever you do, do it out of love, respect, and honor to the mom and dad who adopted you. Don't act out of a sense of insecurity about a past that could disappoint you.

Dear Pat,

I have a really bad temper. I always feel sorry after I've exploded at someone, but I keep doing it. Do you have any suggestions?

The Human Volcano

Dear Lava,

I have a bad temper, too. It's embarrassing, isn't it? I once got angry with a guy for beating me at a video football game. I shoved him into a closet. I think that was the last game we played together.

Get your Bible out and open it to Luke 9:51-56. This is a story about a couple of guys with bad tempers. Jesus was going to visit a Samaritan village, but He wasn't allowed in. So two guys, James and John, asked Jesus for permission to command fire to come down from heaven and destroy that village. Whoosh! Crispy critters everywhere. These were men of God who were asking to do this. In fact, John is the author of the fourth Gospel and Revelation.

Jesus said no to them. He didn't lose His temper with the village. Why? He was secure in Himself and His mission on earth. He knew He would be attacked at times. He knew He wouldn't always be liked. He didn't care about winning or losing.

Why do we lose our tempers? It's usually because of pride. We think someone is putting us down or trying to take something away from us. The next time you feel that anger welling up inside, stop and say: "God totally accepts me and loves me. I can afford this hurt without getting uptight about it." Think about Rom. 8:18. Then relax and let your friend out of the closet.

Dear Pat,

Is the female moustache a curse
from God?

Fuzzy Lips

Dear Lips,

Yes, it is. Gross, isn't it? You can't even drink milk
without that white mark settling in among all that
friendly fur.

When Adam sinned, he not only guaranteed a
life of sweat and toil for all of us (Gen. 3:16–18), he
also went from being God's blessing to having an
imperfect body. So welcome to the joy of:

sweaty palms
bony knees
crooked noses
stray nose hairs
hips that spread forever
no eyebrows

Is there hope? Yes.

And even we Christians, although we have
the Holy Spirit within us as a foretaste of future
glory, also groan to be released from pain and
suffering. We, too, wait anxiously for that day
when God will give us our full rights as his children, including the new bodies he has promised
us—bodies that will never be sick again and
will never die (Rom. 8:23, LB).

Until then, find a guy who's farsighted and quit
drinking milk.

Dear Pat,

My dad is always critical of my athletic performance. No matter what I do, he has some negative comment. Why?

A Poor Sport

Dear Sport,

There're a few different possibilities here. I'm going to trust that you can figure out which one is the truth.

Does your dad criticize everybody? Check it out. Does he rip on everything? If he does, it reveals that he's not happy inside. If he's not happy on the inside, nothing will make him happy on the outside.

Is your dad mostly critical of athletes? This could be happening for one of two reasons. Maybe he was a great athlete, and he can't stand imperfection in others. Maybe he was a so-so athlete (or one who had a career-ending injury), and he's living his life through sports today. Every time an athlete (or you) fails, he is failing all over again.

Your dad may think he is motivating you He may already believe you're a great athlete but that you need mental toughness, fine tuning, and a little humility. If that's the case, you need to tell him that you like compliments, too. Be honest with him. You're not an athletic machine; you're his son.

Remember, with all his weaknesses, he's your dad. So respect him.

Dear Pat,

The big thing with my friends is comparing our after-school jobs. It bothers me that I don't make as much money or have the kind of job that my friends consider classy. Is it wrong to feel that way?

Job Nerd

Dear Jobbed,

I'm glad that we didn't compare jobs when I was in school. I used to drive a snow cone truck. For ten cents you could get cherry, lemon-lime, or grape. Ding, ding, ding, ding! Our motto? "We freeze it; you squeeze it!"

The truth is that I made more money than the so-called prestige jobs, but my hands were always cold. But I enjoyed my work. That's the key.

What you feel is what a lot of adults go through every day. They're always looking at other people's jobs and wondering why theirs isn't as great as their friend's. Your after-school job is not a measure of you as a person. Your after-school job is something you're doing to make a few bucks and learn to be on time (well, sort of).

Enjoy it. Don't compare it. Do your best until it's time to do something that doesn't involve grease. If people say that we're supposed to be judged by where we worked during our high school years, then they're dingier than that bell I was ringing.

Dear Pat,

Last year I was all league in football. I was also very popular. This year I'm not doing so well in either area. Was I accepted because of my ability?

Former Most Valuable

Dear FMVP,

Everyone loves to be around a winner, but real friends don't care about scoreboards. Men in high school, such as yourself, shouldn't be impressed by the scoreboard either.

When I first started speaking, I got a lot of praise for the way I communicated. I thought I was pretty hot stuff. I forgot it was God who was gifted. I had fallen in love with His gift and had forgotten about Him. All of a sudden, boom! I was "All Pro" one minute and under the bench the next.

It happened on the road to Dallas. I got really sick. This wasn't a case of indigestion; it was a result of spiritual nerves. I had lost my faith in God, and I was scared. I had lost more than if I had lost all my friends; I had lost my best friend. Jesus was nowhere to be found. I felt so alone. I had a great prayer time that night, and He assured me that I should never judge myself on my accomplishments—or by my "friends." His grace was enough for me.

In a way, I'm glad you're not a great football player this year. It may make you appreciate a great God instead.

Dear Pat,

I have a real hard time accepting compliments. Why?

Don't Like Myself

Dear DL,

It's very simple: you don't believe nice things about yourself. You probably think you're an okay person but no big deal, right? Well, here's a new belief system for you.

Step one: Your value is not based on past shame, it's based on glory (2 Cor. 4:7—memorize it!) Jesus Christ has been spiritually planted in your imperfect body. He has replaced your weird personality, your negative thoughts, and all your bad experiences with His glorified Spirit! You're no longer a loser.

Step two: Be excited about the fact that you're God's perfect child in every way You won't always feel perfect (there will be zits once in a while, etc.), but God doesn't recognize body shape or our personal insecurities as anything that makes Jesus less perfect in us. You can hold your head up high.

Step three: When someone compliments you, realize they're recognizing God's life through you You can respond now by saying, "Thank you. That was a very nice thing to say." In your heart, you can thank Jesus Christ for making you so valuable.

Dear Pat,

I'm anorexic. Why?

Skinny Minnie

Dear Minnie,

You're not anorexic! You have chosen anorexia as a way to feel better about yourself. It's a trap. It may feel good for a while, but in the end it can only mess up your body systems and possibly kill you.

Recently I spoke at a high school in southern California, where a fifteen-year-old girl had chosen to be anorexic. Her skin was literally turning green. In her efforts to be "thin," her body didn't stop at the normal boundary. Her rib cage was protruding, and she finally consulted her doctor. He told her: "You've got to start eating normally again. If you don't, your heart won't withstand the pressure you're putting on it. You've chosen anorexia. I want you to change your choice. I want you to eat!"

She went on a supervised diet. I admired her convictions. She realized she could do something about her problem. She started eating healthfully again, and the color came back into her face, but she had a heart attack and died three weeks later. Most of her school came to her funeral. Everyone had the same thought: "You didn't have to be thin to be our friend. We liked you just the way you were!"

Get some help from a counselor and a doctor, Minnie. Your life is too important for you to choose self-destruction. Don't wait another minute.

Dear Pat,

I have trouble believing God really accepts me. Why is it so hard for me?

                    Feeling Unloved

Dear Loved,

There are several possible reasons why you have trouble understanding God's love.

Your earthly father didn't show love Where do we learn about God's acceptance on this earth? From our parents. If we had a father (or a stepfather) who didn't love us unconditionally, then it could be hard for us to think God does love us. Solution? Don't judge God by your father's inability to love.

You haven't really read the Bible Read Romans 8 over and over again. Discuss it with a mature Christian whom you trust. The Bible doesn't lie. It'll tell you the truth.

Quit trusting your feelings so much Just because you don't feel loved doesn't mean that you aren't loved. If you believed donkeys could fly, would that make it true? Of course not! Just because your feelings say, "I don't think God accepts me" doesn't mean you have to listen to them. Tell them to grow up and get in touch with the Bible.

Don't go on past experiences; look at Christ's experience Jesus died on the cross because He was worthy in God's eyes. He transferred that worthiness to us. That's called "grace." Every time you think of yourself as a failure, thank God for His grace. It says more about how lovable you are than your mistakes do.

Dear Pat,

My boyfriend always makes cutting remarks whenever we play any sports together. I know I'm not as good as he is, but I like to play. Can you help?

No Gold Medalist

Dear Goldie,

So your boyfriend thinks you don't measure up very well on his territory, huh? Well, why don't we show him the other side of life.

Let's say you were really good at music. You won awards for music. You could play any instrument without much practice. Your boyfriend, on the other hand, couldn't tell the difference between a tuba and a trombone. If you asked him to accompany you at a recital as your musical partner, how would he respond? Can you say "scared spitless"? I knew you could!

There are things we can do well and there are those other things. Your boyfriend is not good at everything he does, and he *knows* it. That's why he needs to be patient with others in areas where they're weak. If he's not, he better learn to play some games that require only one participant. These are lonely sports.

You spend time with someone because you like that person, not because you're equal in ability. If there're some games you can enjoy together, then so be it. If not, both of you need to decide if your boyfriend understands patience. It's spelled h-u-m-i-l-i-t-y.

Dear Pat,

As a high school student, I find
it very difficult to relax. It's
really a problem for me.
Suggestions?

Uptight

Dear Uppie,

It is very important that you get to the heart of
this problem. Why is it so hard for you to relax? Here
are some possibilities.

Feeling pressure from either parent? Someone
sets standards for us, and if we don't feel able to meet
those standards, it could make it difficult for us to relax. Are either of your parents uptight most of the
time? Do they set really high standards for themselves
and for you? Your answer is likely right here.

Misplaced goals? Sometimes we strive really
hard to accomplish a goal that's impossible to attain.
For example, I could hope to be Miss America, but
I'll never make it. If I were a perfectionist, I could
get more and more uptight. This ongoing frustration
will give me no rest. Are your goals frustrating you?

Lack of scriptural depth? The Bible constantly
tells us to relax in Jesus Christ. He died on the cross.
We don't have to climb up on one and do it better
than He did. Do you really believe you can trust His
completed goal for you eternally?

Constant sense of failure? Sit down with a
Christian counselor and share your real feelings
about yourself and your view toward past failures.
It's possible that those unfulfilled accomplishments
are convincing you that you're not a successful person. That makes it very difficult for you to relax.

Dear Pat,

I lie constantly. Why?

Dishonest

Dear Dizzy,

When you were a kid, did you ever eat all the cookies in the cookie jar? Does that sound familiar? Did the ensuing exchange sound something like this:

Mom: Did you eat all the cookies?
You: Uh . . . what cookies are you talking about?
Mom: You know what cookies I'm talking about!
You: No, I don't!
Mom: Are those crumbs on your face?
You: No (quickly wiping them away), they're freckles.
Mom: Are you lying to me?
You: Um . . . uh . . . well . . . not really . . .
Mom: Look me in the eye!
You: (Squirming to avoid looking)
Mom: You ate them, didn't you?
You: I'm allowed one phone call, aren't I?
Mom: Who're you going to call?
You: Judge Wapner.

Why do we hide the truth? Why do we always want to look good? If people really knew the slime ball inside us, would they really like us? Paul said, "Yes, all have sinned; all fall short of God's glorious ideal; yet now God declares us 'not guilty' of offending him if we trust in Jesus Christ, who in his kindness freely takes away our sins" (Rom. 3:23–24, LB).

The battle's over, pal. As a Christian, you can start telling the truth. You're totally accepted, no matter how gross you feel.

Dear Pat,

I want to be a millionaire by the time I'm sixteen. Is there anything wrong with that?

Into the Bucks

Dear Alex,

There's nothing wrong with your plan, especially if you're my business partner. If that's your *goal*, however, there's something wrong with it.

Making money is not an end result for a godly man or woman. Our goal should be summarized by the following verses:

You cannot serve two masters: God and money. For you will hate one and love the other, or else the other way around.

For the love of money is the first step toward all kinds of sin. Some people have even turned away from God because of their love for it, and as a result have pierced themselves with many sorrows.

(Matt. 6:24; 1 Tim. 6:10, LB)

I suggest you write out the last half of 1 Timothy 6 and put it on your desk as a reminder that money can be a very powerful force in our lives—for good or for sin. Remember: missionaries need money, hungry people and the poor need money, the church needs money to spread the gospel to the world. Use your talents and resources to the glory of God, but don't sell your soul to Satan in the process. Being rich isn't worth that.

```
Dear Pat,

I think a lot about the possibility
of nuclear war. Do you think it
could happen in my lifetime?

        Don't Want to Glow in the Dark
```

Dear Glow Worm,

I don't think nuclear war is a strong possibility. Anything is possible, but before we have a nuclear war we have to have nuclear enemies who are capable and willing to engage in that kind of war. Our first choice is probably the Soviet Union. But it's not likely that the Soviets would get into a nuclear war with us. Why? Several reasons.

Their economy is very unstable They really can't afford a war!

They need us to survive If they nuke us, then they won't be able to take advantage of our resources. No United States, no bread on their table.

They're already overextended In case no one noticed, the Soviets pulled out of Afghanistan for the same reason we pulled out of Vietnam; they're having problems at home and they need to cut back on their "world domination."

They're chess players, not bombers The Soviet Union historically only fights wars that they can win. If they see the possibility that they can't checkmate someone quickly, then they'll play defensively and safely. When confronted by a power equal to them, they back off. Nuclear war with us is not their style.

China looked like a threat in the 1960s and 70s, too; until President Nixon negotiated a major breakthrough in our relations with them. They, like the Soviet Union, seem to be moving toward a system more similar to ours than to the one they've had since Mao. These two countries are not our best friends, but they seem to be more interested in making money and stabilizing their economy than in nuking us or anyone else. I also see them opening their doors to allowing the Gospel more freedom in their country.

I favor a strong national defense, but not just because of the Soviet Union or China. Those are not the countries I worry about. My concern is for the smaller nations like Libya or Iran. They don't seem to care for human life. They're capable of making some kind of nuclear strike in our direction, but their air forces and our more sophisticated defense systems keep me sleeping at night. I hope by the time they have the capability to bomb us, their leaderships will have changed and mellowed to the point where they care about the futures of their countries and all the lives they could affect. They could not defeat us, but they could mess up a few cities and wipe the smiles off Mount Rushmore. If we retaliated (and we would), it would be the last thing they did for a few hundred years.

I was born three years after we dropped "The Bomb" on Japan. I remember 1962, when we stored our food for a potential war with the Soviet Union, and a few neighbors actually dug underground shelters. I think we were much closer to a nuclear war at that time than we are now. I don't see the end of the world in the near future, not because I trust other nations, but because we continue to have a strong defense. That's better than my Teddy bear!

PAT HURLEY is well known across the United States and in Canada for his humorous messages in high schools. Since 1970, Pat has appeared at more than three thousand schools and before more than 3 million students and parents.

From 1980 to 1982, Pat was the resident comedian on ABC-TV's "Kids Are People, Too!" In 1982 he received an Emmy Award for his hosting of a teenage talk show in Los Angeles. In 1988 he received a second Emmy for a similar show in Chicago.

Pat is now syndicating two shows for teenagers, one on television and another on radio. He is the author of five other books and has produced or appeared in nine films, including *Friends Are Friends Forever*, being distributed by Word, Inc.